D1575321

# LIGHT BULBS FOR LEADERS

# $\mathcal{P}$RAISE FOR *LIGHT BULBS FOR LEADERS*

There cannot be a successful organization in America today that doesn't depend upon teamwork for superior performance and growth. During a time when rapidly shifting societal and economic changes are scrambling conventional notions about personal interactions, *Light Bulbs for Leaders* is the perfect descrambler. Its technical approach is the right mix of creativity, boldness, and scar tissue, all presented in an arrestingly readable package.

Norman R. Augustine
Chief Executive Officer
Lockheed Martin Corporation

This "how to" book provides helpful, practical insights into the complexities of teams and teamwork. It is an attractive and handy compilation of notes and guidelines which any busy manager can relate to, with a rare discussion of the nuances of individual differences . . . that in reality can make or break an effort for team building.

Walter F. Ulmer, Jr.
(Former) CEO and President
Center for Creative Leadership

*Light Bulbs for Leaders* is a truly powerful book for teams and leaders. It captures those behaviors that are so important, but are often forgotten in the rush of working together. *Light Bulbs for Leaders* isolates the behaviors so that leaders and teams can use them as needed. It is a practical and useful tool. I keep it in my briefcase and refer to it often.

A. Sims Cooledge
Vice President, Organization and Leadership Development
Scudder, Stevens & Clark, Inc.

The findings published in *Light Bulbs for Leaders* are an interesting, lively, and very readable treatment on the topic of leadership. Like *In Search of Excellence*, the material has a curiously inspirational quality which is particularly compelling. This book should be essential reading for those in positions of leadership and those aspiring to be—a welcome, well-founded book on the topic.

Dan DeLapp
Human Resource Department Manager
ARCO Alaska, Inc.

*Light Bulbs for Leaders* is pithy, practical, and easy to get your arms around. Unlike the typical academic psychobabble, this book is straightforward and clear. It provides activities which are an ideal method to build the working relationships required in today's changing and complex organizations.

Todd S. Greenberg, Psy.D.
President
Prescience, Inc.
Lecturer at Harvard University

Most of us are convinced that good teamwork can make our companies more successful. But how do we get there? That's the beauty of *Light Bulbs for Leaders*. It takes complex ideas and makes them simple—easy to understand and easy to follow. Inspiring examples and clear principles make this a dynamite guidebook for leaders and teams.

Kevin R. Daley
President
Communispond, Inc.

*Light Bulbs for Leaders* with its "Guide to Team Learning" is a practical and useful addition for any manager's skill set. The lessons are particularly noteworthy for their simplicity and practicality. These lessons are as good a set of guideposts as I've seen.

Phil Melita
Director, Organizational Development
Life Technologies, Inc.

What a thrill! Received *Light Bulbs for Leaders*. . . . It appears the book's focus is on cooperation and collaboration in the workplace, and I couldn't agree more that both are absolute necessities, especially between teams in the same organization.

Don Pratt
President
Praxton Enterprises

I finished *Light Bulbs for Leaders,* and it has helped me to reflect upon some very important things that I had not been paying enough attention to in my work, but should have. It is a good reference guide, once someone has a basic understanding of leadership and teams. . . . I have been given responsibility for planning and implementing some major changes involving my school in the next academic year. I'm glad that I will have *Light Bulbs* at my fingertips. Some of them have lit up for me already!

Allan J. Futernick, Ph.D.
Associate Dean, School of Criminal Justice
Rutgers University

*Light Bulbs for Leaders* is a great read for CEOs and anyone who wants to get a quick overview of essential aspects of leadership and team formation. Ideas pop out and lights go on. It is an important reference book for trainers and consultants interested in the development of learning teams.

Elaine Biech
CEO, ebb associates
Author of *TQM for Training*

*Light Bulbs for Leaders* is a must read for team leaders and team members alike. By applying the ideas in this book, any team can experience improved results.

Richard C. Whiteley
Vice Chairman
The Forum Corporation
Author, *The Customer Driven Company*

An excellent, practical, and useful tool for the modern workplace.

Hyler J. Bracey, Ph.D.
CEO, The Atlanta Consulting Group
Author of *Managing from the Heart*

An excellent book . . . on leadership.

The Honorable Ike Skelton
4th District, Missouri
U. S. House of Representatives

*Light Bulbs for Leaders* is two books in one—a compelling story of the lessons we can learn from organizational life and a leadership handbook on how to guide teams along the path to performance. It's a delightful read about a subject made boring by far too many. Plug into this tale of teams and leaders and *your* light bulbs are sure to gleam.

James M. Kouzes, coauthor of
*The Leadership Challenge* and of *Credibility*
Chairman and CEO
Tom Peters Group/Learning Systems

This book describes a fictional group of senior managers who try to turn their organization around in response to declining budgets and increased competition. The managers learn to motivate their workforce, change an ingrained culture, and employ a collaborative, cooperative leadership style rather than their customary command-and-control style.

—*Training* Magazine
Lakewood Publications
March 1995

*Light Bulbs for Leaders* is two books in one. The first begins with an extended fictionalized case study illustrating key lessons in team growth patterned on the forming-storming-norming-performing model. The second examines team-learning principles. The book is based on previously available work, but the synthesis is original and worth a look for those grappling with team implementations.

Theodore B. Kinni
*Quality Book Digest*
March 1995

Show up, be present, tell the truth, and let go of outcome. Those are just some of the principles on leadership in *Light Bulbs for Leaders*, a book by Barbara Pate Glacel and Emile A. Robert, Jr. The book—by VIMA International—follows the activities of a high-performing team at the fictional Fulcrum Corporation through the stages of group development: forming, storming, norming, performing, and adjourning. Readers can learn from the team's experiences. The guide addresses such areas as feedback, communication, checklists, and the assessment of team behavior.

*New Training Tools*
Training & Development, January 1995
American Society for Training and Development

# LIGHT BULBS FOR LEADERS

## A GUIDE BOOK FOR TEAM LEARNING

Barbara Pate Glacel

Emile A. Robert, Jr.

John Wiley & Sons, Inc.

New York • Chichester • Brisbane • Toronto • Singapore

This text is printed on acid-free paper.

Copyright © 1996 by VIMA International, Inc.

Published by John Wiley & Sons, Inc.

All rights reserved. Published simultaneously in Canada.

Reproduction or translation of any part of this work beyond
that permitted by Section 107 or 108 of the 1976 United
States Copyright Act without the permission of the copyright
owner is unlawful. Requests for permission or further
information should be addressed to the Permissions Department,
John Wiley & Sons, Inc., 605 Third Avenue, New York,
NY 10158-0012.

This publication is designed to provide accurate and authoritative
information in regard to the subject matter covered. It is sold
with the understanding that the publisher is not engaged in
rendering legal, accounting, or other professional services. If
legal advice or other expert assistance is required, the services
of a competent professional person should be sought.

ISBN 0-471-14663-3

Printed in the United States of America

10 9 8 7 6 5 4 3 2 1

Dedicated to Maxwell R. Thurman
General, United States Army
(1931–1995)

A Leader of Teams,
A Teacher of Leaders,
A Role Model for Learning,
Who turned on light bulbs for others in all he did.

With thanks for his friendship, mentoring, and
contributions to leadership and learning.

# $\mathscr{A}$BOUT THE AUTHORS

**Barbara Pate Glacel,** Ph.D., is chief executive officer of VIMA International in Burke, Virginia. Dr. Glacel consults in executive and organizational development for organizations such as Lockheed Martin Corporation, NASA, MCI Communications, Atlantic Richfield Company, Life Technologies, and various organizations in the United States, Europe, Africa, and the Pacific Rim. She is an adjunct faculty member at the Center for Creative Leadership.

Previously, Dr. Glacel was general manager of the Management Programs Division, Hay Systems, Inc., member of the Hay Group of Management Consultants.

Dr. Glacel has been an assistant professor of business and political science at the University of Alaska, Anchorage, Central Michigan University, the University of Oklahoma, and other colleges. She is currently on the Alumni Board of Directors of the College of William and Mary. She serves as vice president of the Instructional Systems Association.

Dr. Glacel holds a Ph.D. in political science and an M.A. in human relations, both from the University of Oklahoma, and an A.B. in government from the College of William and Mary. She is a published author in the fields of organizational culture, quality, leadership, and public policy analysis. From 1986 to 1990, she was a member of the U.S. Army Science Board, advising the Secretary of the Army on human resource issues. In 1995, she was appointed by the Secretary of Defense to the Defense Science Board Panel on Quality of Life.

**Emile A. Robert,** Ph.D., is chief operating officer of VIMA International in Burke, Virginia. He has over 20 years of experience in human resource development and administration. He is an acknowledged authority in organizational development, personnel assessment and evaluation, forecasting human resource needs, and professional development.

Dr. Robert has worked as an executive development consultant for Hay Systems, Inc. He has served as deputy director, Executive Development Office of the National Defense University, and associate professor of leadership in the Department of Behavioral Science and Leadership of The United States Military Academy, West Point.

Dr. Robert works with clients across the United States and in Scotland, New Zealand, Southeast Asia, and South Africa. He is on the adjunct faculty at the Center for Creative Leadership.

Dr. Robert holds a B.S. in engineering from The United States Military Academy, an M.A. in sociology from the University of Pennsylvania, and a Ph.D. in organizational behavior from Yale University.

# $\mathscr{F}$OREWORD

Last count, I am told, there were 478 books on leadership listed in *Books in Print*. Yikes! Even half that many is enough to discourage anyone from putting pen to paper—or fingers to keyboard, as the case may be. Why on earth do we need one more book on team leadership? Why on earth should you read this one?

I'll tell you. Between the covers of *Light Bulbs for Leaders* you'll find more essential and practical advice on what you can do to improve how you lead teams than is between the pages of 90 percent of all those other books combined. Besides, it'll take you a lot less time.

Barbara and Chum are very astute. They know that most of us learn how to lead from the trial and error of our own experiences. So what do they do? They begin by treating us to the modern-day tale of a very believable team of managers learning as they go—with all the fits and starts, tensions and conflicts, successes and failures of real organizational life. I got the eerie feeling I'd been at this team's meetings. You will, too.

But Barbara and Chum know that experience is the best teacher *only if* we learn from it. So the characters in the story take time out to "chart the group's learnings." (It's something every team *should* do, but most don't.) The Fulcrum managers find 88 lessons from their experiences—if I counted right—63 about teams, and 25 about leaders.

They could have stopped there. After all, some of the best-selling business books have offered us stories and lessons. But

Barbara and Chum added something else very special that alone is worth the price. They added extra value by including a book within a book showing how to learn from team experiences. In their "Guide to Team Learning," you'll find a treasure trove of tools and techniques that you can actually try out. There are surveys, checklists, tips, and questions—one-stop shopping for team leadership.

Of all the principles and practices that Barbara and Chum offer, one hit me between the eyes. All exemplary leaders have internalized it, and without it nothing else matters. All the 88 lessons are worthless unless leaders take to heart Barbara and Chum's first principle: "Show up: You must be present to influence others." Obvious, right? But how many leaders do you know who think they can influence people from the 52nd floor of a gleaming tower, or from an isolated corner of headquarters, or from behind the closed doors of their office, or by hanging out only with people just like them? "Show up" is such a powerful first principle because we only come to trust our team members and our leaders if we get to know them. And we can't get to know them unless they are there, unless they are present. Woody Allen said that "80 percent of living is showing up." Well, with apologies to Mr. Allen, I think when it comes to leadership, 98 percent of leading is showing up. Strategies don't matter, visions don't matter, values don't matter, nothing else matters unless you show up.

And one final point—and the thing I love most about *Light Bulbs for Leaders*—Barbara and Chum don't treat leadership with reverence and awe. They don't complicate it, and they don't mystify it. They remind us that leadership is a set of skills and practices that—*if* you take the time to learn and use them—will improve the effectiveness of the groups you lead.

Myth associates leadership with superior position. It assumes that leadership starts with a capital "L," and that when you are on top you are automatically a leader. But leadership is not a place, it is a process. It involves skills and abilities that are useful whether one is in the executive suite or on the front line, on Wall Street or Main Street. If there is one singular lesson about leadership from all of the research my colleague, Barry Posner, and I have done over the past 15 years, it is this: *Leadership is everyone's business.*

Fortunately, *Light Bulbs for Leaders* does not perpetuate this myth. Instead, it offers us a refreshing look at what a team just like yours can do if you take the time to learn from your experiences. *Light Bulbs for Leaders* goes on my short list of recommended reading for all new and experienced leaders alike. Make sure you include it on yours.

Jim Kouzes

San Jose, California

# $\mathcal{P}$REFACE

Teams come in assorted shapes and sizes, for various purposes, with different ground rules, but the very popularity of the word in 1990s organizations gives us the impression that "team" is synonymous with "good." In truth, however, teams are nothing new. They're organizational groups capitalizing on the athletic team analogy.

Teams may go the way of the quality movement—just another "flavor of the month"—if we don't look at what makes them work, where they work best, and what effort is required to truly get team commitment, synergy, and productivity. A group of people does not a team make. A high-performing team, much like a good relationship, requires communication, commitment, behavior change, and continuous feedback. All of these activities are hard work and require skills that are not easily learned within the context of a business crisis. They are better learned within the context of everyday work of learning teams.

High-performing teams are not ends in and of themselves. They may not be the best forum to complete all organizational work. But, where teamwork is required, the teams must be focused on achieving corporate goals and objectives, rather than becoming the goals themselves. Teams are only as good for the organization as the quality of the work they produce.

In our work with high-performing teams, we find that successful ones must learn the lessons of team development and continuous learning for themselves. Our assistance comes in pointing out to them when certain inevitable activities are taking place. As team members begin to view their own process, learnings dawn on them: light bulbs turn on. In the story that follows, you may see your own team in action through the experience of a high-performing team at the Fulcrum Corporation. This team of senior managers is charged with a very real task: turning the corporation around in the face of declining budgets and increasing competition. That scenario is not uncommon. What is uncommon is their attempt to carry out this task as a learning team, the very foundation of a learning organization. Their experience puts some of the lessons about teams and leaders into context for your better understanding.

Follow the activities of this high-performing team that travels through the stages of team development: forming, storming, norming, performing, and adjourning. What the team experiences is that team learning is not a sequential, lock-step process, but consists of continuous learning. Sometimes, the same lessons are learned over and over within different contexts, without ever reaching the perfection of high performance for all time. Rather, each time the team meets, it must go through the preliminary forming process yet again as it improves its ability to learn from experience and to perform at higher levels of excellence.

Once having made the journey as a high-performing team of peers, the Fulcrum managers must lead the team learning process in their own organizational teams. This transition requires that they lead in a more hierarchical setting. Some light bulbs remain the same; others are different when team learning is implemented by the organizational leader. As you continue following the activities of these managers, you will experience the context for light bulbs about leadership in a team environment. Perhaps these learning light bulbs will help you review your own team process, allowing you to learn the lessons of experience about team performance.

All of the lessons, of teams and leaders, are captured in a sequential model following the story of Fulcrum's managers. Real life, however, is not so sequential. The Fulcrum high-performing team must "muddle" through its own task in order to learn from experience in a more scattered, yet realistic sequence. The sequential model will help you understand where lessons fit within the team development stages; don't expect, however, that you will experience them in the same order. In fact, the nonsequential lettering of the light bulbs will remind you that the team at Fulcrum learned their lessons in a variety of situations, not in a lock-step process.

To gain the most value from *Light Bulbs for Leaders*, the reader is encouraged to read the fictional story with an eye for the familiar. When do these same frustrations and roadblocks get in the way of performance in your organization? The characters who lead the effort at Fulcrum may be fictional characters, but each of them is cloned many times in today's organizations. As they strive to motivate an intelligent workforce, to change an ingrained culture, and to operate through cooperation and collaboration more than command and control, they often find themselves venturing into the unknown. What seems to be a straightforward task is fraught with the roadblocks of human behavior.

By describing this adventure into the unknown within a context, the reader may more readily understand how difficult team leading and learning really are! As you encounter the problems of this learning team and the leaders who must implement change, think about what skills are needed to complete this task. How would you perform under such conditions? When is team cooperation and collaboration necessary for successful completion of the task? What are the roadblocks that your team encounters? How do they compare to those problems stated in the Problem Matrix on page 88?

To help you learn the lessons of leaders and teams, and to practice the skills necessary to lead this team effort, the "Guide to Team Learning" provides a concise explanation of the primary skills for learning through team development. These skills are the basis for learning new and creative ways to operate, to create synergies from differences, and to change the very nature of the way we work in organizations today. The skills must be practiced, refined, improved, and consciously demonstrated in order to become a daily pattern of one's learning behavior. Only then will learning teams be more than a buzzword and will roadblocks become movable.

The Problem Matrix will help you identify potential behaviors to break the roadblocks for your team development. As you consciously try out the new behaviors, be sure to vary your approach until you have practiced all the necessary skills and can use them with more comfort and less contrived introduction. By then, you will have them at your disposal and can use them when needed in order to create true learning teams.

Barbara Pate Glacel
Emile A. Robert, Jr.

Burke, Virginia
April 1996

# $\mathcal{A}$CKNOWLEDGMENTS

This book is about leadership at all levels and the practice of leadership in teams that are devoted to continuous improvement. To write this book, we observed countless leaders and learning teams practicing those skills that make them successful. That practice may be far from perfect. The dilemma for leaders is that their practice field is not hidden from public view, but is right out in front of the followers, the organization, and other observers. So, the best of leadership comes from both successes and failures along the way.

Our thanks go to all those leaders and teams who invited us to coach them and to observe their march toward high performance. We are particularly indebted to our clients and colleagues at The MITRE Corporation who work with us on a long-term project with learning teams. We have learned from them, even as we have opened their eyes to the importance of leadership and learning processes.

The challenge for us as "experts" is to practice what we preach. The team of leaders at VIMA International is diligent in its efforts for continuous improvement, exercising leadership at all levels, and keeping the titular leaders humble! Our gratitude and appreciation go to Obie Braaten, John Dold, Gretchen Hannon, Linda Harrison, Sharron Lamkin, Katharine Long, Diane Rice, and Patricia Ryan. On a daily basis, they are the epitome of a learning team. On this project, they spent countless hours in the production and publication of this book. Our thanks and love go to each one.

The original version of *Light Bulbs for Leaders* was a self-published edition. We learned a great deal about the publishing industry as we struggled through the project in all its phases. Our thanks go to our coaches along the way, especially to Ray Bard at Bard and Stephen, Jack Covert at Schwartz Business Books, and Ted Kinni at The Business Reader. An inspiration to us and a true leadership guru is the author of our Foreword, Jim Kouzes. Thanks, Jim, for your leadership challenge! Finally, our editor at John Wiley, Janet Coleman, deserves special appreciation. Thanks, Janet, for recognizing our potential, seeking us out, and motivating us to a higher level of excellence in creating this edition of *Light Bulbs for Leaders*. You are a joy to work with!

Finally, our thanks go to our families who challenge us daily to share leadership and to learn as a team. During this project, they also endured our diversion of focus, our prolonged work hours, and our fascination with the fictional learning team which became our work. To Carol Robert and Bob Glacel, we give our love and thanks for supporting us every inch of the way. To Jennifer, Sarah, and Ashley Glacel and Emilie Stephano, Janis Harral, and Sherri Stadtler, we appreciate the leader and the love in each of you.

BPG
EAR

# CONTENTS

## Book III
## A Guide to Team Learning

# Book I

# *A* Tale of Teamwork and Continuous Learning

# THE CHALLENGE

THE CEO, GARY ANDERSON, was very concerned. In the past, customers had come to Fulcrum willing to pay high prices for the breakthrough technology that was Fulcrum's forte. The technical brilliance and superb reputation of Fulcrum's employees had made the company great.

Suddenly, it seemed, that was no longer the case. But, as Gary looked over the statistics of the past several years, he could actually see the erosion of Fulcrum's position as first and best in the marketplace. As technology became more widespread and more competitors could do the same good work as Fulcrum, customers were not willing to put up with high prices and sometimes less-than-cooperative consultants. Gary knew that a real culture change was the only solution to Fulcrum's problem and the key to survival.

At Fulcrum, information was power. The scientist or engineer who knew the most about a given technology could control the projects worked on, the status of both projects and people in the organization, the schedule of deliverables, and the "lifestyle" at work. Therefore, information was not shared freely. The organization was full of brilliant "cowboys" who worked well independently but resisted efforts to collaborate. The result was redundant silos and skunk works, which delivered technological breakthroughs but were inefficient. The engineers and scientists who gave Fulcrum its technical edge were abominable businesspeople.

Budgets, marketing, customer service, and deadlines on product deliverables were anathema to their creative minds.

Gary was convinced that the survival of Fulcrum was dependent on sharing information, working more synergistically in teams, eliminating duplication, and learning to be more efficient and cost-conscious. Gary decided he couldn't save the company by himself. He had to enlist the help of middle management. He wanted to deliver a wake-up call to his managers, but he wasn't sure how to get them to buy in to the seriousness of the situation. He was honest and direct as he addressed the company directors, laying out the gory details and telling them that they must work as a team to come up with a plan to save the company. If the organization was to survive, productivity had to increase. No ifs, ands, or buts; the directors were in charge of restructuring Fulcrum to position it in the marketplace they faced today, not the marketplace of their comfortable past.

Most of Fulcrum's 32 divisional directors shared Gary's concern. They weren't quite sure how to go about working as a team, but they were worried enough to believe they couldn't go it alone anymore. On the other hand, they knew that 32 was too large a group to get anything done. Six of them, all peers in the organizational structure, volunteered to form a Productivity Team:

JANICE  an up-and-coming young technical director who was acknowledged as a role model for women at Fulcrum.

TED  one of the old-timers at Fulcrum who had been around but continued to learn new ways of doing things and loved the new technologies.

PAT  a real go-getter who was a workaholic and technical expert and had been at Fulcrum for about ten years.

ANDY  the human resources director who frequently had to hold the hands of the technical managers and their staffs when people problems cropped up.

JOHN  the corporate communications director who had to speak for the company and occasionally tone down others' arrogant words.

LOIS   a technical director who was hard as stone and didn't understand why people couldn't just work together to get the job done and leave all their idiosyncrasies behind.

The team came together for their first meeting and immediately struggled with the questions: Why are we here? What do we do? How do we proceed? After an hour of no progress, Andy called a break. On the way to the bathroom, John suggested to Andy and Ted that lunch be brought in. "It's already 11:30," he said, "and we have a long way to go." The three agreed. As John spoke with his secretary to make the lunch arrangements, Ted told the others about their plan.

Janice said, "That's fine with me, but I have a 1:00 P.M. meeting that I can't cancel. I promised an hour and a half to this team, but I have a real job, too."

Pat said he had a lunch meeting and wasn't interested in the typical sandwich and chips from the dining room. Lois mumbled something under her breath that sounded like a cross between, "I can't stay either" and "Why aren't you as dedicated as I am?" At this point, John stepped in, saying catering couldn't respond in 30 minutes. All orders for takeout lunch have to be submitted in triplicate by 4:00 P.M. the previous day.

"Herein lies our primary problem," challenged Pat. "We're so tied up in red tape, we never get anything done together. I'm outta here. Someone call me when you figure out what we're supposed to do and what you need from me." The others were discouraged.

Lois broke the silence. "I've been taking notes. I suggest that I write up the minutes and send them to everyone on E-mail. When can we get back together again for an hour?"

"Based on today, I'd say an hour isn't long enough," returned Ted. "Let's start at noon in my conference room, with lunch, and go as long as it takes to make some progress."

"We have to put an end time on the meeting because I have to coordinate child care with my wife," said Andy. The five agreed on a 5:00 P.M. stop time and found a day the next week when it was possible to meet. John agreed to tell Pat of the plans.

# ℱORMING THE TEAM

THE FOLLOWING WEEK, the team was scheduled to reconvene. Lunch for six arrived at Ted's conference room as requested. The cart bearing sandwiches, chips, drinks, and cookies was Ted's second reminder of the meeting, his secretary having mentioned it earlier that morning. "Where has the morning gone?" wondered Ted. "For that matter, where is everyone else?" Just then, Janice, Pat, and Andy turned the corner.

"I picked these two guys up in the lobby. Neither could remember where your area was," Janice said. "I guess we should have the corporate headquarters weenies in our area more often."

"Don't call me a corporate weenie," was Pat's return comment. "I can't help it if headquarters happens to be located where my work is. Besides, it isn't any fun traveling to get here. If we need another meeting, you guys can come to us."

"Where's John?" Ted asked.

"He was scheduled on the same flight we were," answered Andy, "but Gary needed to go over his next article in the *Fulcrum Flyer,* so John couldn't make it."

"What's the article about?" asked Janice.

Pat responded, "The CEO is going to announce what we're up to with respect to gaining more synergy, efficiency, and all that dribble."

"Is Lois coming? I've got 20 past 12:00."

Ted told the team that Lois had left a message for him: she had to meet a client downtown this morning and might be a little late. He suggested that they go ahead and start lunch without her. Soon Lois showed up and joined the others. She came into the conference room to hear chatter about sports, the latest gossip at Fulcrum, and kids' school activities. After saying hello, Lois remained silent while the conversation ranged far and wide. Finally, with some frustration in her voice, she exclaimed, "Can we knock off the small talk? I would like to finish what we need to do on this committee and get on with important projects."

"Well," responded Pat, "Andy and I were talking on the flight down. We agreed that the minutes you wrote up were great. Neither of us thought we had made any progress at all last week, but that wasn't the case. We may be nearly done."

Andy jumped in, "I do agree that we made progress, but I think we have a long way to go before we can recommend anything to Gary. I think it would be useful to take a minute and have each of us tell the others why we're here."

"Did you read all the way to the end of my minutes?" Lois asked. "The last page is an agenda for today, and telling each other why we're here isn't on the agenda."

Ted, who had been sitting thoughtfully, asked, "Do you mean why we are here today, or why we volunteered to join the committee?"

"Well, I guess why we joined in the first place."

"I don't understand the purpose of this exercise, but I put my hand up because I've been thinking about this sort of thing for a long time. Every successful organization I read about talks of sharing more information than you could believe and using high-performance teams and things like that. I kept asking myself, 'Why couldn't we do it at Fulcrum?'" was Janice's rather impassioned offering.

"I sort of joined for the same reasons," said Pat. "I also figured that you and I, Janice, share a lot of technology with different clients, and I thought this might be a way for us to work more closely together."

"Oh, for goodness' sake, Pat, tell the truth," Lois challenged. "You were afraid Janice would get ahead of you in terms of brownie points with Gary."

Pat deflected Lois's challenge by asking why she had volunteered. She said, "I don't know. I think when I saw that Andy and John were both part of it, I was afraid we would end up with some sort of sappy idea that just wouldn't work in operations. I wanted to guard against that."

"That really hurts, Lois," was Andy's reply. "I'm here because I heard Gary talking about teams, even though he didn't use that exact word. I know some things about team development and thought I could help with the process this team would have to go through."

"Fair enough, Mr. Process Expert," Ted was speaking again. "I've noticed you taking a lot of notes; how are we doing so far?"

"Well, I do have some process observations I'd like us to discuss, but we still don't know why you volunteered to be a part of this team, Ted."

"I joined because you don't have to be CEO to realize Fulcrum's in trouble. There are a ton of competitors out there scratching for work. They have very smart people and are both hungry enough and have deep enough pockets to wipe us out. I think we have to get our act together quickly, or fold the tents and go home. This exercise strikes me as one of survival, more than just another of Gary's pet projects. Now, what are those process observations?"

"Are we ever going to address my agenda?" lamented Lois.

"That's one of the observations I have," answered Andy. "The idea of setting an agenda and following it is critical to meeting management and also raises the question of team leader. Who's in charge of this team anyway? And since no one paid attention to Lois's earlier comment about her agenda, have we just wasted three hours of our meeting time?"

"I certainly don't think it's been a waste of time," responded Janice. "I'm fascinated with Pat's suggestion that this team may help him and me work more closely together."

"I'm also concerned that Lois seems to think we are in some sort of a 'suck up to Gary' contest with each other," added Pat.

"I'm confused about the scope of the project we have. Some of you seem to think we will be done today, but Andy's comments make it sound like a project requiring several months. What's the truth?" challenged Ted.

"The truth is," said Lois, "I'm sorry for the catty remark to Pat. I really didn't mean it. I think I said it because I was frustrated that you all seemed to blow off the agenda I had really put some time and thought into. I do hope you guys can work together more because I think it will not only help what you do, but also serve as a model for the rest of us. Finally, I share your concern about how big an elephant we have to chew up in this project. Frankly, it worries me to think about having a meeting like this once a week for months on end."

"I've been studying Lois's agenda and thinking about how to proceed with this task," said Ted as he went to the white board. "Here's how I see it. . . ." During the next hour, the team reviewed Gary's charge to them and decided what additional data they needed, how they would gather the data, and when they would meet again.

Pat was amazed at the progress they had made in such a short time but complained that meetings at Fulcrum always seemed to go like this. "If we had gotten down to work at noon instead of griping at one another for a couple of hours, I could have made the early flight home," he complained.

"Do you agree with that assessment, Andy?" asked Ted.

"Not really," Andy responded. "You see, the team development literature tells us that teams typically go through stages of development. The first is *forming*, where boundaries are being formed and members are asking themselves questions about the cost of membership and whether they will be accepted."

"Acceptance is never an issue for me," Lois retorted.

"I'm sure you're right on a conscious level, Lois, but unconsciously the question does come into play. That may be one way to understand the catty remark to Pat, for which you later apologized."

"Wow! You *have* been watching the process," marveled Janice. "What happens after the formation stage?"

"Once individuals accept membership, they enter the *storming* stage. It's called storming because individuals are concerned about what they do and are trying to be sure others in the team don't step on their toes. It's best understood as *turf battles*."

"It really felt like a fight a little while ago when we were deciding who was going to speak with which corporate officers and with our peers about this task. Was that an example of storming?" Ted asked.

"Yes, and there were other examples, too," Andy answered. "After the team succeeds in passing the storming stage, it enters the *norming* stage, where the questions of how we conduct ourselves, and who is responsible for what, are agreed upon more openly. It's here that trust begins to be developed. The team can then *perform*, which is the next stage, and really begin to produce synergistic work."

"So," concluded Pat, "since we've formed, stormed, and normed, we should have a dynamite meeting in two weeks and produce some great results, right?"

"Well," Andy went on, "not exactly. That's one of the real traps people fall into. They think team development is a linear process, but it isn't. A team will find itself almost invariably redoing each stage every time it meets. Not only that, stages are entered and left somewhat randomly during every meeting. The better we are at verbally recognizing what's going on within the team, the better we'll be at getting our work done."

"How do we verbally recognize our stages?" asked Lois.

"We use a technique called *process checks*. We stop the content discussion and check out with one another what is really going on. We examine the process we are using to see if it is helping us or getting in the way of our achieving the goal. For example, when we have a discussion and hidden agendas get in the way, we say things that we don't really mean—like your comment to Pat. You could think about comparing what is being said with what you feel in the pit of your stomach. What your stomach is telling you reflects the things that are most important internally, or what you are really thinking. If your gut feel is very different from the words being said, it's time for a process check. Probably other people are feeling the same way, and the meeting needs to come back to open and honest dialogue and working toward the goal. Remember, though, getting comfortable with each other is part of working toward the goal."

"So process checks are a useful tool for each of us to use when we get together?" Lois checked.

"Exactly," returned Andy. "Can I record that as a team learning that resulted from this session?"

"Sure," said Janice, "but I think you're forgetting something that may be important. If I understand this forming stage, it's where boundaries get formed. In other words, we know by the boundaries who's in and who's out, right?"

Andy smiled, "That's great, Janice; yet another learning."

"Well," Janice responded, pleased with her correctness, "what about John? Is he or is he not a part of this team?"

"Of course he's part of the team. I've missed his insights today," responded Ted. "Andy, can you bring him up to speed about what we've done and what we want from him at the next meeting? Will you also tell him that his penance for not being here today is to host the next meeting? One thing we didn't decide on was where it will be held."

"Hold on." Now it was Pat's turn to join the conversation. "It sounds like you expect John to buy what we've done here, hook, line, and sinker, and punish him for not being here, to boot. I suggest that Andy brief him on both our progress and process so far. If he has alternative suggestions, he can voice them on E-mail to everyone. That way, he'll feel more in the loop. As for the next meeting, I'll host it in my conference room, and the logistics won't have to be changed."

"You're right, of course, Pat," was Ted's reply. "I just wanted to yank his chain a little. Thanks for hosting the next meeting. We'll see all of you in two weeks."

# Storming

THE TEAM CAME TOGETHER in Pat's conference room, wondering how "touchy, feely" this next session would be. When they had left the last meeting, Andy's observations seemed to make sense. But, in the light of the real world of operations and keeping up with clients' needs, the process and team development observations Andy had talked about seemed worlds away. There was just a bit of discomfort as the six came together, this time with John in attendance.

Pat was the host of this meeting, and he asked who would like to scribe and who would be the leader for the agenda. It seemed that this team of peers had difficulty in accepting a leader for the team. No one person wanted to be self-assertive in front of the others, but they all jockeyed to be the keenest and most insightful in the process. As the discomfort became palpable, Andy interjected, "Perhaps we should recap where we left off at our last meeting, especially since John needs to get up to speed with the rest of the team."

When no one accepted the challenge, Andy continued. "John, we accomplished quite a bit on task, especially in terms of who would do what, where we would search for information, what our time line might look like, and when we would produce results. But, we also talked about how we would work together as a learning team. Perhaps by reviewing our process, we can articulate some behaviors that would help each of us individually as technical or staff directors, too. Can you guys help me with your insights on our process from two weeks ago?"

Lois jumped into the fray. "Well, John, I had sent out an agenda on my E-mail to everyone, and it sure took a long time for us to get to the topics. It seems we had to go through some kind of getting to know each other. I really wasn't much interested in whose kids did what at school, but Andy said that was important."

"Yeah," Ted chimed in. "And I tried to stick you with hosting the next meeting, John, to punish you for jumping ship for our last meeting. But Pat saved your skin on that account."

As everyone laughed, the discomfort eased, and Andy began charting the team learnings.

## Process Learnings for Effective Teams

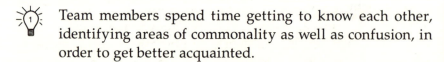 Team members spend time getting to know each other, identifying areas of commonality as well as confusion, in order to get better acquainted.

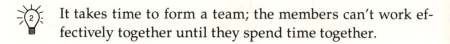 It takes time to form a team; the members can't work effectively together until they spend time together.

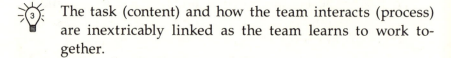 The task (content) and how the team interacts (process) are inextricably linked as the team learns to work together.

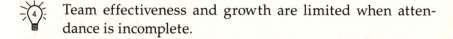 Team effectiveness and growth are limited when attendance is incomplete.

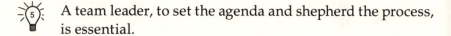 A team leader, to set the agenda and shepherd the process, is essential.

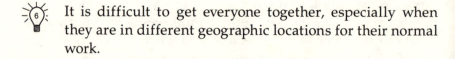 It is difficult to get everyone together, especially when they are in different geographic locations for their normal work.

Team activity must compete with other high- or higher-priority initiatives, but developing effective teamwork must be seen as a legitimate activity that is essential to good task and organizational performance.

 Teams need both experienced and inexperienced members for reasonable diversity, a sense of ownership, and mutual accountabilities. A team is more than a collection of people; it is a process of give and take.

By now, Lois was getting impatient. "OK, Andy, so we've charted all these learnings. Now can we get on with things?!"

"Sure," Andy replied. "Who's in charge?" The silence that followed showed that something had been left hanging at the previous meeting. Pat had agreed to be in charge of logistics, but no one had taken responsibility for the agenda, as Lois had done at the previous meeting. Not wanting to appear ill-prepared, each member jumped in at once with something unique to add.

"Well, I really think we need to go to Gary right away with our discussions," Janice chimed in, and the one-upmanship started.

About 45 minutes later, Ted asked quietly, "On a scale of 1 to 10, with 1 being low, what is your assessment of the likelihood that we'll ever get anything coherent to Gary?" After a few minutes, the team realized Ted was serious and wrote a number on a slip of paper as he had requested of them. Ted collected the papers, computed a quick mean, and announced that the mean response of the team was 2.2.

"So what?" Pat said angrily. "That's just confirmation to me that it's an impossible task. If this weren't my area, I'd probably have left by now. As it is, I'm thinking about resigning from this team."

"In answer to your question, Pat, I don't know 'what,'" returned Ted. "I've been trying to figure out why my gut feel doesn't match what we're all doing right now, as Andy suggested. I can't put my finger on it. But I still had to say something. I have a sinking feeling we're getting nowhere fast. Do you have any ideas, Andy?"

"No ideas, but, as you may have suspected, some observations."

"Go right ahead, Andy," Lois said in disgust. "I'm off to the bathroom while you take your process time-out. I'm sure I'll be back before the real work starts again."

"I could use a break, too," John stated. "Let's all break for ten minutes. I disagree that Andy's observations aren't real work. It's beginning to feel like they tell us what's hard about working in a team."

Everyone agreed, and the team reassembled in ten minutes. As Pat came in, he announced the news of an unexpected snowstorm. "The office has been closed. My secretary was waiting for us to break so she could tell me she was leaving," he reported.

"Leaving now is really not very helpful," John observed. "Traffic will be a real mess. I find that waiting until 8:00 or 9:00 P.M., when the plows are out and traffic is lighter, makes more sense for me. Of course, I get a little hungry by then, and the snack machine is always out of candy bars."

"Lois, Ted, and I flew in today and planned to spend the night, so it really doesn't matter to us. We can walk across the parking lot to our hotel," Janice said.

"*Trudge* looks like a better description of what we'll be doing to get there," commented Lois in a much quieter and more conciliatory tone, as she stared out the window. "I hadn't even noticed that it had started to snow. The folks here don't have much of an idea of how to deal with the white stuff, do they?" The break and this new event seemed to have mellowed Lois. She continued, "If you guys are able to work it, why don't we spend a little longer here, and then all go to the hotel for dinner together? That plan might make this process check requirement more palatable to me."

Pat, Andy, and John checked with respective loved ones and confirmed that everyone at home was safe and secure. When they came back, the other three were just finishing packing the flip chart and markers. "We decided to hear your process observations in the lounge of the hotel, Andy," reported Ted. "The snow isn't getting any less deep in the parking lot, so it would seem that the sooner we leave, the better."

# NORMING

THE HOTEL ACCOMMODATED THE TEAM with a quiet space in the dining room where they could work. After ordering, it was Andy's turn. "I only have two observations so far. The first is that, whenever someone asked who the leader for this session was, the question was completely avoided. The second is that we have spent the majority of our time so far announcing conflicting conclusions from the data we collected. No one has said anything about what the data were that led to those conclusions. It's almost as if each of us thinks the others will automatically agree with what we say. Both observations are clear examples of the storming phase of team development."

"I could buy that—if it were true," challenged Pat. "You're obviously leading now and did at the beginning of the meeting, too."

"Yes and no," said Ted. "Andy's leading now and did at the beginning, but I think all the avoidance of the subject came when we were trying to get into the content part of our work. Even if we accept that what he's talking about is important, it's way outside our area of expertise and has little to do with what we tell Gary."

"Why does it have so little to do with what we tell Gary?" This came from Janice who had silently gone halfway through her dinner in deep thought. "It seems to me that sharing information, working synergistically, eliminating duplication, and learning to be more cost-conscious and efficient has more to do with process than our own technology."

"I agree, Janice," said John. "That's what all the people I've spoken with were telling me. Our technology is fine. What we need to do at Fulcrum is quit worrying about who gets the credit, and other concerns that don't add value."

"I think we should follow Andy's advice and publish the data each of us has," suggested Ted. "Why don't you start, John, since it's on your mind?"

Sometime later, Lois said, "It's amazing what a change in atmosphere can do. I never thought we'd get to so much agreement. The funny thing is, while what we've decided is quite different from what I had in mind, I like it much better. Can we reward ourselves with dessert?"

Pat chimed in, "Wow! I agree on all three points. I was ready to give up earlier, I really like what we have, and I'm ready for dessert, too. Are we a team yet?"

"Probably," said Andy, "but one thing still worries me. We have accomplished a lot, but we've still avoided the leadership issue."

"I've been wondering about that, too," Janice joined this line of thought. "I'm not sure I'm authorized to make process observations, but it seems to me that at different times during the conversation, different people have been leading. It sounds trite to say, but leadership seemed to rotate."

"I agree." Now it was John's turn. "I don't think we've avoided anything, Andy. Record as a process learning that in effective teams, leadership rotates. The person who has the most passion about a particular topic will jump up and grab the pen and take charge. That's what's been happening here, and we are feeling great about what we've done."

Andy went to the flip chart, turned to a clean page, and wrote, "Process Learnings" at the top. Opposite the first bullet, he wrote, "In effective teams, leadership rotates."

"What if there isn't any passion?" asked Ted.

"Oh geez! I was just getting excited about process," lamented Lois. "Are you suggesting that if no one has passion, nothing will get done? We obviously can't have that at Fulcrum. Lots of the stuff we do is drudgery born of bureaucratic regulations. No one has passion for that junk."

"I wasn't sure," returned Ted. "Now that you've said it like that, I guess that's more than what I was thinking. What was in my mind was the fact that we had a harder time getting started today, in part because we didn't have an agenda. You had done an agenda for the last meeting as part of the minutes. This time, Andy just wrote up the minutes. No agenda. I guess no one had passion to do it, so it didn't get done. We didn't define that responsibility at our last meeting."

"But this is phony," said Pat. "When I hold a meeting, I have a published agenda because I know what I want to accomplish."

"What's phony about this team, Pat?" Andy asked.

"Perhaps *phony* is the wrong word. We are all peers, for openers. High-powered peers at that. We respect each other's abilities so much, no one has wanted to step forward and appear like a dictator." As Pat spoke, the team could almost see the light bulbs starting to illuminate in his head. He went on, "The result was that we took a while getting started. We spent a lot of time going over what we had done in the first two meetings, and finally got to the point of making progress very late in this one. What I wonder is how much the change in atmosphere contributed to our success."

"The change in atmosphere helped us move a mental roadblock," offered Ted. "This meeting seemed very un-Fulcrum-like. What bothers me most is that we got so much done once we got around to it, and we all feel so good about the outcome. This result also feels un-Fulcrum-like."

While this conversation had been going on, Andy had been quietly adding more learnings to the chart. Now it looked like this:

## Process Learnings for Effective Teams

 In effective teams, leadership rotates.

 The person with passion for a topic assumes leadership for that topic.

Leadership is important for continuing focus and progress of the team.

 It is hard to keep a team focused.

 Any change in team membership means a new beginning of team formation issues.

 There is more information and knowledge within a team than is usually revealed.

 Team members need to build trust in a safe place, to get to know each other. This happens most easily in a job-neutral environment away from organizational interruptions and repercussions.

 Learning to relate to each other takes time.

 Time must be allotted for wide-ranging discussion to scope a problem to manageable proportions; this requires patience.

 Talking about the team task is easier; talking about the process of working together is more difficult.

 Team members need to stay process-vigilant. Each member must be allowed to call a process time-out (process check) without penalty.

 Avoiding both the issue and the leadership for the issue is a common practice in ambiguous situations.

 The team should capture learnings by reflecting on the team process at every meeting, either before beginning the content discussion or at the end of the content discussion—

or, preferably at both times. These learnings should be *published* and considered equally valuable to the content actions taken.

 People do things, teams don't. Therefore, leadership is required in teams.

"What's the last item about, Andy?" asked Janice.

"It just popped into my head. Lois and Ted were saying we got things done in spite of not having a leader, but we had an awfully hard time doing it. It occurred to me that, unless we assign responsibility for what's needed, it may or may not happen. The way an organization gets around that problem is to hold a person accountable. We typically think about that person as the leader, who occupies a fixed position. I think what the learnings say is that sometimes it has to be that person and sometimes it doesn't. There may be an official leader assigned to head a team, but it's much easier to decide who the leader is at any one time if one forgets about a fixed position in the organization. There are other criteria for leadership in a team besides official position.

"Perhaps our difficulty has been that we occupy the same position relative to each other. What I'm wondering is: Why do I have the impression that Ted has been the one who consistently brings us to focus on the task, whether it's process- or content-related?"

" 'Why' is not worth wondering about as long as we focus," responded Ted. "Besides, dessert sounded like an awfully good idea to me several minutes ago. Let's order. We can wrap up the remaining details for our next gathering while we enjoy our dessert."

They did just that. Janice would host the next meeting. They agreed to begin with a dinner meeting on the night before a morning meeting to be held a week from today. Lunch would mark the wrap-up. To deal with the leadership issues, John agreed both to publish the minutes from the present meeting and to propose an agenda for next week's meeting. In the meantime, everyone would think about the direction they were heading and come prepared to discuss those thoughts over dinner.

# $\mathcal{P}$ERFORMING

"I CERTAINLY ENJOYED LAST NIGHT." Lois beamed to everyone in general as she swept through the conference room door right on time.

"The rest of us were just saying the same thing," Pat replied. "We have a dilemma now, though. Janice ordered the coffee and sweet rolls yesterday. They've arrived right on time, but her secretary just came in to say Janice was involved in a fender bender on the freeway."

"Was she hurt?" Lois was genuinely worried.

"No one was injured," Pat continued, "but the police are there, and it'll be a while before she can get the mess sorted out. To make matters worse, Ted was summoned by his VP this morning to solve some customer problem. What can we do until those two arrive?"

"Janice will probably be here in an hour, but I doubt we'll see Ted at all today," offered John. "I wonder if we can make some tentative progress on the agenda based on the conversation last night, and then bring our absent members up to speed when we do meet them. Are you willing to try?"

The four members present agreed to start. After all, they had spent a good portion of dinnertime last night going over the thoughts each one had about the results of their work. It was about 9:15 A.M. when Janice finally appeared, looking a little haggard.

"Are you OK?" Pat was the first to speak.

"Oh, I'm fine," Janice responded. "There really was no major damage to anything or, thankfully, anybody."

"What took so long?" asked Lois. "Frankly, I was really getting worried."

"There were three other people involved and a couple of police representing the 'county's finest.' I stood back and marveled at how none of those individuals would listen to the others. I even thought about trying a process time-out once, Andy, but emotions were running too high."

As the others had a hearty laugh imagining Janice calling time-out at a traffic accident, Pat sat deep in thought. "I've just been thinking," he mused. "Every time things really got hot in this team, we had to take a break to get back on track. Is that typical of teams, Andy? Was Janice's problem this morning that there was no way to take a break? Can we generalize from that learning?"

"*I think so, probably,* and *yes,* if I have the sequence of your machine-gun barrage of questions in the right order," Andy replied. For some reason, Janice was able to stay out of the emotional flow of the group on the highway and see what was happening. If she could have gotten people to stop for a moment and just think, things would have gone more smoothly. I hadn't thought about it, but when a team takes a break, it gives the members a chance to disconnect emotionally from the situation. Used judiciously, it's a good technique to get a team back on track."

"What an opportunity!" exclaimed John. "Let's take ten minutes, refresh our coffee, and then bring Janice up to speed on what we've been doing."

When the team reassembled, Pat asked to take the lead in explaining what had transpired in Janice's absence. Pat's stepping forward pleased the others, because he had been fairly silent during the proceedings. He explained to Janice that Lois and Andy had started storming on the technology-versus-people issue, and that John had done a masterful job of summarizing their respective points and getting each to listen to the others. "I assigned myself the role of making sure the comments you and Ted made last night, as well as my own thinking, were well represented," he concluded. "How did we do?"

"I don't know what the storming was about," returned Janice, " but the outcome looks excellent to me. I have one question about . . . ," and the team was back into the task on which they were rapidly approaching a conclusion.

Hours later, the arrival of lunch was a welcome sight to the team. The two white board walls were filled with data and decisions. Lois summed up the feelings of everyone by saying, "We've covered so much ground this morning, I'm feeling a little confused. Perhaps we should spend some time hearing a comprehensive summary."

"That's an excellent idea, Lois. I'll get started consolidating on the flip chart while you're getting your sandwiches," John suggested.

John did just that and then helped himself to lunch. As he sat down, Ted arrived. The process used to inform Janice was repeated for Ted from the viewpoint of both process and content results. After having several questions satisfactorily answered, Ted suggested their product looked ready to present to Gary. They easily agreed on task assignments for this event, as well as the need for one last look just prior to getting onto Gary's calendar. John had phoned Gary's secretary and was told that the only time available during the next month was late afternoon on the following Thursday.

"Guys, I hate to say this, but I have a meeting scheduled in about 15 minutes," lamented Pat. "I thought the time would be safe, but we've already gone a couple of hours beyond our scheduled end time."

"What about our process learnings?" Andy asked with some disappointment in his voice.

"I guess you could go on without me," Pat responded sadly.

"As important as those learnings are, I'm afraid they'll have to wait," added Ted. "I have to do some follow-up on my crisis of this morning. Is it possible for each of us to make some notes on what we observed from both last night and today? Then, perhaps we could have dinner together next Wednesday evening with process learnings as one agenda item. On Thursday, we could spend some quality time making sure our presentation to Gary is crisp."

Everyone agreed to this plan, and the meeting adjourned.

# $\mathcal{L}$EARNING

THE TEAM GATHERED FOR DINNER the next Wednesday evening. As the meal was winding down, a lapse in the conversation occurred. Andy broke the silence with one of his annoying statements of the obvious.

"It feels uncomfortably silent all of a sudden," he said.

"Our verbal agenda has process observations as the item of business for the evening," was the curt response offered by Lois. "I don't know who's leading this session, but he isn't being active enough for me at this point. I hate to say so, but I really want to get on with our business. Enough chitchat, if you don't mind."

"We didn't appoint a leader for this session," exclaimed Pat, slapping his forehead. "This team stuff isn't so hard, we just keep forgetting our past learnings. Whose fault is that?"

"Fixing the blame doesn't help us make progress," Janice stated with conviction. "Since we've identified the problem, I suggest we turn to our process expert and ask Andy to take charge of the session and get on with it. What do you say, Andy?"

"I think using a flip chart or white board to record the learnings is more effective because everyone can *see* what's being said, as well as hear it. But in this place, I guess a pad of paper will have to do. I suggest each of us state one process learning from the last meeting or this one. I'll record each one and, whenever necessary, do a summary. If that's acceptable to everyone, I'll list the first learning, which I just picked up: Fix the problem, not the blame."

"That's abusing the power of the pen, Andy, but we'll let you get away with it this time. I have a couple of other learnings to add," chided Ted.

Each in turn listed process learnings. The ideas of one person sparked comments, thoughts, and ideas from others. It was all Andy could do to keep up with the team. Finally, there was a pause in the verbal input.

"Did you get all of that, Andy?" Lois asked.

"I think so," was his reply. "I'm glad I got one learning on the list before you all started, because you stole all my other good ideas. This was exciting and profitable, I think."

"Indeed it was," agreed Janice. "Can we wait until morning for a detailed summary? I think I'd be fresher then. I also need to call home to say good night to my son, and I think I'd like to take advantage of the balmy evening to take a walk before turning in early."

"I'd like time for a stroll, too." agreed Ted. "The weather here is certainly changeable. One meeting, we're snowbound. The next, it's like a spring evening."

"OK," Andy responded. "See you at around 8:30 A.M. in my area. That will give me time to make my notes coherent and readable."

"Thanks for doing that work, Andy," Lois added. "I appreciate your willingness both to keep us on track and to make some readable sense out of all our technocratic bumbling. See you in the morning."

With echoes of Lois's comment all around, the team departed for the evening. When they arrived at Andy's area the next morning, they found this flip chart waiting for them:

**Process Learnings for Effective Teams**

 Fix the problem, not the blame.

 Setting an agenda is important.

A team leader is essential.

 Leadership evolves as a team's needs change.

 Teams develop in predictable stages.

 Teams start the formation stages over at each meeting.

 Process interventions are useful when done properly and with regularity.

 Extra effort is required to bring new people in or old members back in.

 Teams of four to six or six to eight people are a good size: No one can hide, attendance of each member is important, and leadership is shared.

 Team-building is required before the team can be effective.

 Teams get a lot done when they're out-to-lunch.

 Mutual respect, willingness to listen, and trust come only after much work together.

 Working on a real task with a clear outcome is a requirement to coalesce a team.

 Teams function best when their task is not too specific and they can explore their direction together.

It is hard to schedule meetings for all to attend.

 Responsibility falls on all team members to bring people into discussion and to listen to ideas opposite from their own. In other words, all members share responsibility for leadership.

 Team efforts are an investment in the organization's future in multiple ways (e.g., solving problems and increasing networking to promote information sharing, skill building, leveraging experience, and wise use of people's time and energy).

 A person can work on only so many teams at once.

The five assembled members stared at the list. Some were in total agreement, others had questions, and all wondered where Andy had disappeared to. He had obviously been here doing the list earlier this morning. He heard the questions concerning his whereabouts as he came through the door.

"Coffee is served, ladies and gentlemen," Andy beamed. "I just confirmed that I had a dedicated admin person to help with any paper production we might have in preparation for the session with Gary this afternoon. What do you think of our list?"

"We mostly think it's fine," replied Ted, "but you have a little explaining to do."

"What do you mean, 'Teams get a lot done when they're out-to-lunch'?" continued Pat in a challenging tone.

"Lighten up, Pat," Andy pleaded. "We spent a lot of time praising ourselves for the good work we did at the hotel during the snowstorm, at the restaurant before our meeting last week, and again last night. That was just my way of saying it."

"OK, I guess a little humor is acceptable," Janice chimed into the conversation. "What do you mean by the next bullet? 'Mutual respect, willingness to listen, and trust come only after much work together.' I respected everyone here before we started. That's one reason I felt optimistic about the team from the beginning."

"I contend that we've taken respect, willingness to listen, and trust to a different and deeper level," countered Andy. "I realized those were mostly my words when I wrote them, but last night when all of you joined Lois in saying thanks, I had a really warm feeling of respect and trust for each of you. I'm sorry if it sounds sappy; I respected you before, too, but not the way I do now."

"It doesn't sound sappy to me." This reassurance came from Lois. "What Ted and I were worrying about were the next two items. 'Working on a real task with a clear outcome is a requirement to coalesce a team' and 'Teams function best when their task is not too specific and they can explore their direction together' sound contradictory to us. Can anyone help?"

Pat explained, "I had mentioned the 'real task' part, and I heard Ted add the 'not too specific' part later. I asked Andy how he would make sense out of that difference as we drove home last night. We decided that it was true that the guidance wasn't too specific when we started. We, as a team, actually decided what outcome we wanted. There's a little risk in this, which we may find out about this afternoon when we brief Gary, but we provided the specificity. That feels very un-Fulcrum-like. On the other hand, we felt it was critical to our success as a team."

"So," Ted began his summary, "it's the team that provides its own clarity."

"I think that's critical," agreed Andy.

"So far so good, Andy," Lois was speaking again. "However, I don't remember anything at all being said last night about your bullet, that a person can work on only so many teams at once."

"True enough, Lois. I took complete license with the process on that one. As Pat and I drove home, he was mentioning being a part of three other task forces at the moment. This one and two of the others are getting a lot of his attention, but the fourth is really slipping through the cracks. My take-away from that conversation is what I tried to express in this learning. If you don't agree, we can strike it from the list."

"Now that I understand it, I agree completely," was Lois's reply. "Further, since we're recommending this process to Gary both for learning and productivity increases, we're going to have to do more of this rather than less."

"What we're suggesting is really getting scary," John chimed in. "If all of that's true, and the last bullet about team efforts being an investment in the organization's future is true, we all have our work cut out for us. To me, that means we'll have to return to our respective directorates and act in accordance with this list."

"I agree on all counts," said Janice, "but it's a bit scary for me to think about right now. Let's get to our task of briefing Gary."

The meeting with Gary went better than any of the participants could have imagined. He was pleased with their work and charged each of them to replicate their work within their own directorates. John and Andy were further charged to communicate the process and its outcome to the other directors and to begin the task of getting them on board. Gary emphasized the importance of communicating both the content outcomes of the team's work and the process learnings that had evolved. These were as important to the future of Fulcrum's success as were the content actions the corporation would undertake.

# $\mathcal{A}$DJOURNING

JOHN AND ANDY AGREED to draft the report and then clear it with the Productivity Team. That would allow one more opportunity for all of them to get together and celebrate their success. Working with the slides they had used for Gary, they finished the content part of the report with ease. As they pondered the three lists of process learnings, however, they wondered whether all their learnings had been captured. Some overarching learnings seemed to emerge from a review of the whole process. To the list of process learnings, they added some important points.

They also pondered what Gary's charge meant for them: how would they replicate the process within their own teams? Perhaps they should focus on lessons for leaders, which they could share with their colleagues. That approach might allow each of them to "hit the deck running" and avoid relearning each step of the way.

When the team convened one last time, they found a flip chart of more learnings waiting for their approval.

**Process Learnings—A Summary**

 Honest and real feelings expressed by team members help stimulate new ideas. Feelings are valuable data. Being in touch with and expressing what is in one's gut makes a person more "real."

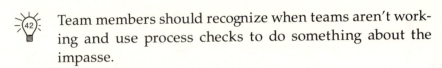

Team members should recognize when teams aren't working and use process checks to do something about the impasse.

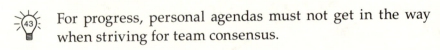

For progress, personal agendas must not get in the way when striving for team consensus.

Effective team performance requires other sacrifices; members should openly acknowledge conflicts and outside commitments.

Team members who expose their vulnerabilities are easier to work with.

Interested members take leadership roles.

Team members express good ideas, have open discussion, listen without interrupting, and accept insights from others. This is helpful in dealing with conflicting views.

Team members need a level of comfort before they are able to trust, open up, vent, resolve conflict, and then function effectively.

The team needs clearly scheduled milestones.

Face-to-face meetings are needed for confronting difficult issues and reaching closure.

The free flow of ideas eats up a lot of time in meetings.

The basis for team performance is the recognition of interdependence; we need each other to accomplish what has to be done.

Collaboration takes a lot of time.

 Communication must be constant.

 Information lives in lots of places one wouldn't expect—inside and outside of commonly held paradigms.

 Teams work if members are committed.

 Commitment leads to passion for the team effort; lack of passion creates a vacuum.

 Delegation allows implementation, but at the cost of control of the outcome.

 To achieve delivery and product integrity, the team must sacrifice. There is never enough time, but the sacrifice must be in proportion to the size of the problem.

 Team learning comes from experience.

 Allocate time for forming, storming, norming, and performing every time the team meets, or pay the price of decreased effectiveness later.

 Team members need training on how to become a high-performing team before they can function as one.

 A team can come to consensus, but may wander in the process.

The team members quietly pondered the lengthy process learnings. Janice spoke first. "There is some redundancy, but I'm not sure it is all bad. One of the things I realized as we worked together is that it is easier to agree to something that I have been a part of than it is to buy in to someone else's work. What I see in John and Andy's list is the result that all six of us produced. I see words each of us used at different times as we formed, stormed, normed, and performed. If we are to publish this list to the other directors, they may identify more with some words than others. I guess that's my long-winded way of saying that the redundancy is OK with me. The list is only a tool—it doesn't have to be perfect if it helps us to be better team members."

John and Andy were relieved that their efforts to be true to their colleagues' words were appreciated. The work of the team seemed complete. It was time to adjourn, yet there was a certain reluctance to leave what had become a team of committed, trusting peers, all working for a common goal. While the six team members lingered over good-byes, they agreed to meet for informal gatherings to share their progress in their own departments.

As they parted, John and Andy shared two more items that could help the directors form their own learning teams. The first, a list titled "Lessons for Leaders" (pages 69–71) would be useful reminders of how to get buy-in and motivation from their own employees. The second, "A Guide to Team Learning" (pages 73–137) outlined the tools they had learned through the experience of spending time becoming a high-performing team.

The team departed with assurances that they would stay in touch as each went about the task of saving Fulcrum, one day and one project at a time. Each member realized that the hard work lay ahead. The months they had spent planning the changes at Fulcrum had allowed them to learn, from their own participation, how to become a high-performing team. They had invested their time, energy, and passion in the effort. Because it was "theirs," they truly bought in, as Gary had hoped they would when he made the assignment. Now, the six directors had to go back to their own work units and replicate the process. How could they convey their own excitement and belief that their plan would work? How could they get buy-in at the next level in the organization and not appear as dictators or, at the very least, messengers with bad news? They were facing a leadership challenge.

# $\mathcal{A}$PPLYING THE LESSONS

JANICE CALLED A STAFF MEETING for the morning after the team adjourned. She had strong feelings about the team of peers who had developed the restructuring plan. She wondered whether she was enough of a leader to pull off the task ahead without that team beside her. As she thought through the demands on her leadership skills that lay in the months ahead, she pondered the lessons the team had helped her learn—lessons about teams and about leadership. The problem was, they all seemed so clear when the team listed them. Janice sat staring at the list of learnings; they were anything but clear now.

**Lessons about Leadership**

 Leaders find that emotion and action are inextricably linked. The passion of commitment is both exhilarating and draining.

 Leaders develop common visions and commitment to the visions by involving those people who work with and around them.

 Leaders must tell the truth as they see it—and then be open for different viewpoints.

 Leaders set clear objectives and milestones.

Leaders focus on excellence.

 Leaders challenge the status quo.

 Leaders focus on the task and include everyone involved in the task.

 A leader's expectation of how another should act affects how the leader treats that person.

 Leaders ensure focus in the process and bring closure when necessary, allowing reasonable digressions.

 Leaders stimulate the free flow of ideas.

 Leaders need to be sensitive to team members' need for feedback, communicating frequently.

 Leaders foster nonthreatening environments where learning and leadership take place.

 Leaders create an atmosphere of trust.

 Leaders create an environment for learning.

 Leaders encourage an appropriate level of participation.

 Leaders are open and inclusive and don't need to run the show.

Leadership can be distributed and shared. In a word, it rotates.

 Leaders look for common ground before trying to resolve differences.

 Leaders deal with different people differently, drawing on the value individuals add, not the differences in personality, behaviors, or experience.

 Good leaders don't necessarily make good members—they have to learn to be members.

 Establishing a leader among a peer group is difficult and awkward.

 Leaders are necessary to team process. Designating a leader is important when responsibility for action must be fixed.

 Leadership is a skill that needs to be practiced.

As she stared, she felt her stomach churn. Her own emotion proved that the first learning was clearly true. Then she thought about the vision of greatness for Fulcrum that had emerged from the Productivity Team. She began to take heart as her eyes flowed over "challenge the status quo" and "focus on excellence." Then the line about "being open and inclusive" caught her eye. She was happy that she had decided to use her large conference room and include all of her managers and key staff members, 20 in all. Her excitement began to build as she got up to meet the group.

Janice started the meeting with a summary of the talk Gary had presented to the technical directors when they first learned of the problems at Fulcrum. Having thus defined the problem, she launched into her vision of greatness. There was plenty of emphasis on excellence and challenge to the status quo. Then she launched into general comments about how this directorate would cooperate with Pat's directorate located at corporate headquarters. Those who shared her passion for the project would form a task force to work out the details for all to follow on this new adventure.

Nearly lost in her own passion for what she was saying, Janice almost missed an audible side comment from one of her most trusted staff members. "What was that?" she asked.

"I said, 'The devil is in the details,'" was the reply from Henry who had been at Fulcrum longer than anyone in the room. "I have to be part of this task force because I have twice as much experience with having cooperation stuffed in my ear by the folks in that directorate. I wouldn't trust them with my worst enemy, let alone the data we're developing out of our latest research effort. This is the craziest idea I've heard in a decade. Don't you directors remember anything about organizational history?"

This comment seemed to start an avalanche of protest and nay-saying. Then, in almost total frustration, Janice called for silence. She redirected the conversation to what they thought was good about the vision. The group began to respond with more favorable comments, only occasionally returning to the original "this isn't the way to do it" line of talk. Finally, George, Janice's deputy said, "I have a suggestion, if it's OK with you, Boss."

"Please go ahead," Janice replied, frustration apparent in her tone of voice.

"I don't know if I have the passion required for this project or not, but I am intrigued by the idea. I'd like a crack at heading the task force. I think Henry should be part of it, for the reasons he stated, and I'm wondering: does someone else really want to be part of it, too?"

Earl, the next oldest staff member in the room and known for his silence, startled everyone by responding first. "I guess I'm on the opposite side of the argument from Henry," he said. "I've been looking for ways to get into the heads of those guys in Pat's group for a long time. I've always thought we could gain by sharing information, so I think I'd like to play in this sandbox."

Two others of the group of 20 also indicated an interest in being part of the group. One more with particular expertise was invited, making a group of six. "I think that's enough for openers," Janice said, reentering the process. "Thanks to each of you for stepping forward. Pat and I have reserved time for a video teleconference to get the process started tomorrow afternoon. George, will you contact Pat's office and see if he has a group ready to meet then?"

"Sure. Can the rest of the team meet me this afternoon at about 3:00 P.M. so we can get our act together before we do the VTC?" Everyone agreed, and the meeting came to a close.

# SHOWING UP

JANICE WAS ALMOST SICK TO HER STOMACH. She hadn't anticipated such a negative reaction. What was wrong with those people? What was wrong with her leadership? Her head was
spinning as she walked into her office, hearing the phone ring on
her desk. Janice turned to her secretary to say, "No calls right
now, please."

"This is probably Pat. He's called three times this morning,"
the secretary said, even before Janice could finish her words.

"OK, I'll take it," Janice said. She suddenly remembered the
agreement with Pat to call as soon as their meetings ended. "He
must have had smoother sailing than I did," she thought as she
crossed her office to her desk and phone.

"Where have you been?" asked Pat. "I was beginning to think
you were avoiding me. Did you have your meeting?"

"I sure did. We just finished this minute. How did yours go?"

"Piece of cake. I called in my deputy, two managers, and one
staff member. I told them we were going to increase productivity
by eliminating redundancies between your group and mine. I appointed the deputy to take charge, told him to get up to four people—he'll need them to help him carry our flag into this
fray—and get on with it starting tomorrow. What have you been
doing for the last two and a half hours?"

"I called in everyone, 20 in all. I told them about the vision of
greatness I had for Fulcrum. I was getting really excited as I

spoke of our focus on excellence and challenging the status quo. Then the storm broke."

"What happened?"

"They told me it wouldn't work and a whole lot more," replied Janice, with much sadness in her voice.

"The problem with you is that you buy into too much of this participation baloney," Pat lectured. "I paid attention to Andy's team dynamics stuff, and it worked perfectly."

"What do you mean?"

"Well, I let them engage in small talk for almost five minutes. Then I cut it off and was the storm myself for a while. When I finished storming, I told them their norm was to go and perform. What they have to do is work out the details, just like we said to Gary yesterday. There were no questions, so I think I led them perfectly."

"Sounds more like you dictated perfectly. Besides, as I learned just an hour ago, the devil's in the details," was the curt reply from Janice.

"Ouch!" Pat said. "Listen, Janice, I really want this to work. I think it's critical, and their commitment is critical. You seem to be saying I didn't get it. Do you think I need to start over?"

"I have no idea, Pat," Janice lamented. "I'm feeling like a total failure myself right now. I guess that's why I sort of snapped at you. George is leading the effort from our end. I've asked him to contact your office and see who our group is meeting with at the teleconference tomorrow. He should be doing that early this afternoon, when he returns from a customer meeting he has to attend. Let's leave things as they are for right now and talk again tomorrow after we get some feedback on how the meeting goes."

"OK," agreed Pat. "I know we share the passion for this venture. Maybe either leadership approach will work. One thing is certain. We'll learn from the process." Both laughed as they remembered their recent struggles at learning from the process, and they agreed to speak tomorrow.

# $\mathcal{B}$EING ATTENTIVE

JANICE FELT A DESPERATE NEED for a cup of coffee. As she turned toward the door, George was standing there with her cup in his hand, full of fresh steaming coffee. "Got a minute to talk, Boss?" was his cheerful question.

"I thought you had a meeting," was Janice's startled response. "Of course I have a minute. How did you know I wanted a cup of coffee?"

"Just a lucky guess on the coffee. As I left our meeting, the customer called and canceled, so I'm left with a sort of free morning. I noticed that you left your notes in the conference room, and I was bringing them to your office when your secretary said you were speaking with Pat on the phone. He can be a pain sometimes, so I got the coffee. Then I was looking over this 'Lessons for Leaders' that was lying on top of your notes. They're pretty good, but I think you left one lesson out. Nevertheless, based on what you have here, I'd say you did a pretty good job this morning. That's what I wanted to talk about."

"Pretty good?" Janice echoed in astonishment. "I was thinking you would be either laughing all the way downtown or looking for a way to bail out of this outfit, based on this morning. What lesson did I leave out?"

"I guess what I was thinking is sort of here. It just needs to be more explicit," George suggested.

 "There are multiple components of leadership. A leader must pay attention to administrative details, must maintain a team focus while being open and inclusive, and must be accountable."

He summed up firmly, "My judgment about this morning was that you did a marvelous balancing act of all of these components."

"Then why was there so much negativity?" challenged Janice. "Why weren't they as enthusiastic as I am? Or was, anyway."

"Please don't lose your passion, Boss. I signed up for the project this morning—and came to work for you several months ago—because of that fire you have. When you outlined your vision and spoke of excellence and doing things differently, I was really excited. When I look down this list, the only way you could have gotten the response you did was by creating, over a period of time, an atmosphere of trust in your team. This morning felt like an environment for learning because you stopped all the negative comments in their tracks and helped us look for common ground. Finding some common ground stimulated a free flow of ideas. All this stuff fits together in fascinating ways. The only downer was the look on your face when you slam-dunked Henry."

"There goes my most dependable engineer. He'll probably never speak to me again. Why did he, of all people, react so negatively?"

"He's not going anywhere. Besides, pay attention, please. The downer wasn't the fact that you did it. The downer was the sad look on your face when you had to. As a matter of fact, his comment was about how much he learns from a good fight like that. It's probably part of his personality. I'd say, going back to this list, that you encouraged an appropriate level of participation by being open and inclusive. You certainly didn't need to run the show. Furthermore, I've always been uncomfortable with the idea of shared or distributed or rotating leadership until I saw you in action this morning. Several of the folks were doing the influencing at different times this morning. When you did the slam to Henry, that's probably an example of focusing the process and bringing closure when necessary. You had already allowed reasonable digressions. Your action brought us all back to the task at hand."

"I felt like a witch telling Henry to stop. I want to apologize to him for that, but he wasn't the only one I told to shut up. Are you saying they all have a personality problem?"

"No, and I didn't say Henry's personality was a problem. There's a learning on this list that addresses that, too. 'Leaders deal with different people differently, drawing on the value individuals add, not the differences in personality, behaviors, or experience.' You crushed Henry, but welcomed other comments with kid gloves. That was brilliant."

"So, if someone agrees with me, I treat them with kid gloves; and when someone doesn't, I slam-dunk them. Some example of leadership that is! It's even on the list," she groaned.

"Boss, you sure are hard to compliment. Do you want me to just shut up?"

"Not at all. I'm enjoying what you're saying, but I still don't understand why everyone was so negative at first. How could that have been prevented? The atmosphere felt threatening to me. What is so threatening about excellence?"

"Nothing's threatening about excellence to these folks. What's threatening is elimination of redundancy. How would you feel if Gary said to you that he wanted redundancy eliminated, and you felt like the redundant one?"

"I never thought about it like that," admitted Janice. "We'd better call them back and tell them their jobs aren't in jeopardy."

"They'll figure that out soon enough," returned George. "Besides, there's nothing anyone can say that will convince them of that. They will have to believe it because of what they see."

"Well, thanks for all your support, George, both at the meeting and in the past several minutes. Perhaps it wasn't a total disaster. Is that the only reason you wanted to talk?"

"Not really. I was hoping for some more guidance about the video teleconference tomorrow."

"I thought I was quite clear this morning," Janice teased. "What more did you have in mind?"

"Just a way to reduce some of the ambiguity, I guess. How much leeway is there really? How much of the farm should we give away? Where do I draw the line?"

"Good questions that I don't think can be answered until we have some options or possibilities. The bottom line is increased productivity, less redundancy, more team work . . . ." Janice seemed to stop in midsentence. She gathered her thoughts and looked George in the eye. "Are you asking me to help you lead our portion of the team?" she asked.

"I hadn't thought about my questions like that," he said. "However, it would be nice to have a little more clarity. As I think about it, I guess I'm having the butterflies you must have felt this morning."

"It's refreshing to hear you say that, George. I was thinking you never had such feelings, given your background and experience. One of the things you will have to do is deal with the establishment of a leader in this group of relative peers, a lesson we have listed toward the end of that list you saw in my notes. As you see in the next-to-last learning, designating a leader is important at some points in the process. The truth is, someone has to be responsible to the team for mundane things like location, time, agenda, appropriate materials, meeting management, and things like that."

"I guess that helps. As it says here on your list, 'Leadership needs to be practiced.' However, no matter how much practice one has, it's still an emotional event to influence others. I'll let you know what happens."

# TELLING THE TRUTH

THIRTY MINUTES AFTER THE VIDEO TELECONFERENCE between the two directorate representatives was to begin, Janice was startled by a rather red-faced George standing in her office door. "What happened?" she asked. "You look like you've been shot at and hit."

"The high point of the meeting was when everyone introduced themselves. Pat's group came prepared with a detailed list of what we should transfer to them and what they were willing to give up to get it. Those guys were vindictive. Henry was the first to say that out loud, of course, but we were all feeling it. I thought the purpose was cooperation. They came in with sharp knives to cut us up. At least that's what it felt like."

"How did it end?" Janice asked. Her voice, calm compared to George's, surprised her.

"You won't believe how childish I was," returned George. "I may have done irreparable damage to the possibility of this project; and if so, I'm prepared to resign my position. I've never felt so stupid."

"What did you do?"

"When they said their director was meaner and stronger than our director, in response to Henry's protest, I pulled the plug."

"I think you need to be specific," cautioned Janice, now very aware of her stomach tightening into knots. "Exactly what did you do?"

"I literally leaned down, grabbed the main power cord, and pulled the plug. Henry screamed that I had just destroyed a million-dollar piece of technology. One of the younger guys restrained him by physically grabbing him and showing how the auxiliary power backup had kicked in. The result was that monetary damage was averted; but, of course, we lost the connection, and I doubt if either group will ever work with me again."

"Where is our group now?" Janice asked.

"They're standing by in my office. I figured you would want to do damage control, and they ought to be handy to make that easier for you."

Janice's mind was racing. George's action was certainly childish. On the other hand, what did that comment about their director being stronger and meaner mean? That didn't sound like the Pat she had grown to trust over the past months. Was she really that naive? Were Pat's words about really wanting this project to work just a smoke screen? She felt anger and fear grip the back of her neck, and she knew that one of those headaches was just around the corner. What had ever made her think she wanted to be a manager in the first place? Taking a deep breath, and consciously relaxing the muscles in the back of her neck, Janice asked herself what action would be appropriate. A dim light bulb was beginning to brighten in her mind's eye. It said, "Process time-out." "How?" she said almost audibly.

"Excuse me?"

"Oh!" Janice seemed startled. She realized that George was still standing in front of her desk. "Ask everyone to come in here," she said to George as she picked up the phone and dialed Pat's number.

# ΒEING OPEN
## TO OUTCOMES

PAT'S SECRETARY ANSWERED THE PHONE after more rings than was Fulcrum's standard. Her tone was more professional than pleasant, and Janice felt the muscles at the back of her neck tighten once more.

"I'd like to speak with Pat," she said after identifying herself.

"I can't interrupt him," was the reply.

"Jane, I've known you for a long time. You really sound nervous. What's going on up there?"

"It beats me," Pat's secretary responded, now in more normal tones, but still agitated. "The morning started with a voice mail message from Pat that he was in Andy's office. I knew he wanted to be around while the VTC was happening, so I called to remind him it started at 9:00 A.M. Old Air Head thought it was scheduled for 10:00 A.M. Honestly, he never pays attention to the schedules I give him. Then I was getting a cup of coffee across from the VTC room, and heard peals of laughter coming from our participants. Just then Pat showed up. His smiles turned to frowns and now they're all in his office. He literally screamed at me to hold his calls and clear his schedule for the morning."

"I've called on the same subject," replied Janice firmly. "Interrupt him now and tell him to pick up the phone. My participants in the VTC are standing in my office, too."

"I think I'm a bit too angry to speak in sentences right now, Janice," was the greeting from Pat.

"Me, too," replied Janice. "However, as I was getting tense, I noticed a very dim light bulb in my head lighting up a process time-out. Can you tell me why you're feeling such anger?"

"I really want a time-out from life at this moment, but let me try to get coherent by talking about my whole morning. Andy and I were riding to work together as usual. He was talking about simpler lessons of leadership he was reading about. He thought we had them all in what we had done, but these had an appeal to him. Thinking the VTC started at 10:00 A.M., I stopped by his office on my way in."

"I could use some simple lessons about leadership about now," Janice said with some hope in her voice. "What's Andy got now?"

"He says there are four requirements. The first is to *show up*. In essence, you have to be there to influence what's going on. Then, to lead, you have to *be attentive*—that is, pay attention to what people are doing. Learn what has heart and meaning for those you're trying to influence. Next, the leader has to *tell the truth without blame or judgment*. Finally, one has to be *open to outcomes*."

"That sounds pretty good, Pat. Are you reading that stuff, or did you understand that much in one short conversation with Andy?"

"First, no one has a short conversation with Andy. Second, yes, I'm reading. Third, I was telling him it doesn't work. You and I both decided not to attend the VTC this morning, but we're still responsible for leading it. On the other hand, my folks are about to hear a large load of truth as soon as you hang up."

"Can we stay with this process time-out for just a bit, please? I was thinking that since there are 11 people listening to half the conversation, perhaps we should get on the speaker phone and model some learning," suggested Janice.

This thought was greeted by a long pause. Janice was aware of her discomfort and that of the others in her office. Finally, Pat replied. "How's this for a risky alternative? A technician just appeared in my office and explained that they have reestablished the VTC link. You want to meet me on the big screen with these folks in tow?"

"Great idea," responded Janice. "We'll see you in two minutes."

As the two groups filed into their respective conference rooms, Janice was the first to speak. "I've been trying to explain to these folks about a process time-out," she said. Addressing everyone, she went on, "When Pat and I were members of Gary's Productivity Team, we used them whenever any of us was feeling uncomfortable with what was going on, or just wanted to be sure we were all understanding things the same way. I admit I was nervous calling Pat to get some data about what happened earlier, but the trust we developed in each other helped overcome that concern."

"The same feeling of trust allowed me to pick up the phone when I was almost too angry to speak," responded Pat.

"What else did you learn at those meetings?" This query came from one of Pat's participants.

Janice responded, "We learned about team dynamics and stages of team development." As Janice went through the four stages of team development, George felt he was beginning to understand his behavior in a different light.

"I guess a VTC setting makes it easier to flee than stay and fight, as I demonstrated this morning," he said when Janice finished.

"I was thinking about that, too," responded Pat. "One of the difficulties I have with the theory is knowing when a team is in which stage. It could be that you decided the cost of membership was too high with my folks carving up your empire, and you just decided not to be a part of that."

Janice chimed in, "The important piece for me is to realize that emotions are going to be happening unconsciously in a team setting. Stopping the content to get at the process is more important than agreeing on what stage of development is 'eating your lunch' at the moment. My people didn't get to hear what you were saying about your leadership learnings from Andy this morning, Pat. Can you review them for us?" Janice asked.

Pat carefully explained what he had said to Janice on the phone earlier. Then, before anyone else could speak, he turned to his group. "The truth for me at the moment is that you completely screwed up our chances for success in this project by not listening to my guidance and working your own personal agendas."

"I beg your pardon, sir." This loud and authoritative offering came from George. "That's refreshing truth for us to hear, but it doesn't seem to fit the 'without blame or judgment' part, and it doesn't sound 'open to outcomes' either."

The silence that followed this remark was deafening. After what seemed like forever, Henry came to the rescue without even realizing it.

"What bothers me is how in the world we got this VTC put back together so quickly," he said.

"That's easy," responded one of Pat's technicians. "But something's still wrong. The audio is clear as a bell, but the video is fuzzier than it was. What's causing that?"

A young technical wizard from Janice's side of the screen said, "I've been wondering about that, too. I think what needs to be done is . . . ."

In the midst of this conversation, Pat caught Janice's eye and motioned to the phone. The two slipped out unnoticed by others in the group who were busy with the content of fixing a common problem.

"On a scale of 1 to 10, what's your estimate of success now?" Janice asked Pat as they met on the phone in their respective offices.

"Well, after such a rocky start, I would have said 2 at best. You brilliantly modeled openness in the midst of the fray. Our conversation may have convinced them of what we really wanted. So, right now, I could be as optimistic as 6 or 7," replied Pat.

"I think you're right. I want to call Andy and thank him for his additions to the list, and get this new information to the rest of our team of directors. I still don't think it's complete, though."

"It's too long already. What do we need to add?" Pat asked somewhat wearily.

"Leadership can be learned. However, it's hard to do because you can't practice in the basement. You have to do it right in front of the people you want to lead."

Janice observed, "You and I are demonstrating that now, at least to ourselves."

"I guess that means we'll have to put up with a little embarrassment as we learn," returned Pat. "I'll call you when I get a report on what our guys have come up with."

# $\mathcal{E}$PILOGUE

WE HOPE THAT THIS STORY has peaked your interest to a level where you are wondering about the outcome. Was the team successful? Was Fulcrum able to save itself? How close is the story line to your own organization? The truth is, we could write whatever ending served our purposes. Because we believe that the lessons about teams and leaders are both valid and important to building a successful organization, we want you to use them. Perhaps, therefore, we should write a very successful conclusion. You could see through that approach easily. Our experience teaches that Janice is correct on both counts. Leadership is a learned skill, and it is hard and sometimes embarrassing to learn because of where one must practice to perfect the skills. Learning to work synergistically in teams is equally difficult. Both difficulties are well worth the effort.

You may have cast your own critical eye on the lessons about leaders and teams, in light of your own personal experience. Are these all the important lessons about teams and leaders? You will probably find one or two that are absent. We are happy to have stimulated your thought process in this regard. And we would be happy to hear your additions to these lists.

Finally, you may wonder whether Pat's approach to leadership was more or less successful than Janice's. Our experience again dictates an ambiguous answer: sometimes it is more successful and sometimes less. It all depends on the leader, those she or he is trying to lead, and the situation or environment within which the influence attempt takes place. Not helpful? We're sorry. The fascination with both leadership and teams comes from their variability.

That does not mean there are no absolutes. We are convinced that, in the long run, paying attention to process will yield results that are superior to those produced without such attention. Any group of people can sprint for a defined period of time. Long-term synergy, however, will be served best (perhaps only) by giving the human processes that happen in teams their due.

The other absolute of which we are convinced is thát, with both leadership and team development, there is no final end-state of success. The processes require continued learning, analysis, adaptation, and improvement. Leadership and team development are hard work, but worth the effort.

# Book II
# The Light Bulbs

The group of managers at Fulcrum learned from their experience: as the situation and context demanded, 88 *light bulbs* dawned on them about working in teams and as leaders. In the story, these light bulbs are numbered in the order in which they occurred. They fit into the two organizing models of this book: (1) the Tuckman model of team development and (2) the four principles of leadership. However, learning through experience is never sequential to any rigid model. Learning through experience is somewhat serendipitous. Therefore, as you review the light bulbs for teams and leaders, you will find that the numbers are not sequential. The numbers refer back to the place in the story in which the learning occurred, and then are placed in the model by stage or principle. The sequence of the light bulbs is less important than the lesson learned.

# $\mathcal{F}$OR TEAMS

## Forming Lessons

 Teams spend time getting to know each other, identifying areas of commonality as well as confusion, in order to get better acquainted.

 It takes time to bond as a team; the members can't work effectively together until they spend time together.

 The task (content) and how the team interacts (process) are inextricably linked as the team learns to work together.

 Team effectiveness and growth are limited when attendance is incomplete.

 A team leader to set the agenda and shepherd the process is essential.

 It is difficult to get everyone together, especially when they are in different geographic locations for their normal work.

 Teams need both experienced and inexperienced members for reasonable diversity, a sense of ownership, and mutual accountabilities. A team is more than a collection of people; it is a process of give and take.

 Any change in team membership means a new beginning of team formation issues.

 Team members need to build trust in a place that is safe for getting to know each other. This happens most easily in a job-neutral environment away from organizational interruptions and repercussions.

 Teams develop in predictable stages.

 Teams start the formation stages over at each meeting.

 Extra effort is required to bring new people in or old members back in.

 Teams of four to six or six to eight people are a good size: No one can hide, attendance of each member is important, and leadership is shared.

 Working on a real task with a clear outcome is a requirement to coalesce a team.

## Storming Lessons

 In effective teams, leadership rotates.

 The person with passion for a topic assumes leadership for that topic.

 There is more information and knowledge within a team than is usually revealed.

Learning to relate to each other takes time.

 Time must be allotted for wide-ranging discussion to scope a problem to manageable proportions; this requires patience.

 Talking about the team task is easier; talking about the process of working together is more difficult.

 Avoiding both the issue and the leadership for the issue is a common practice in ambiguous situations.

 Leadership evolves as a team's needs change.

 Teams function best when their task is not too specific and they can explore their direction together.

 It is hard to schedule meetings for all to attend.

 Responsibility falls on all team members to bring people into discussion and to listen to ideas opposite from their own. In other words, all members share responsibility for leadership.

 Honest and real feelings expressed by team members help stimulate new ideas. Feelings are valuable data. Being in touch with and expressing what's in one's gut makes a person more "real."

 Team members should recognize when teams aren't working and use process checks to do something about the impasse.

 For progress, personal agendas must not get in the way when striving for team consensus.

Effective team performance requires other sacrifices; members should openly acknowledge conflicts and outside commitments.

## Norming Lessons

 It is hard to keep a team focused.

 Team members need to stay process-vigilant. Each member must be allowed to call a process time-out (process check) without penalty.

 The team should capture learnings by reflecting on the team process at every meeting, either before beginning the content discussion or at the end of the content discussion—or, preferably, at both times. These learnings should be *published* and considered equally valuable to the content actions taken.

 People do things, teams don't. Therefore, leadership is required in teams.

 Setting an agenda is important.

 Process interventions are useful when done properly and with regularity.

 Mutual respect, willingness to listen, and trust come only after much work together.

 Team members who expose their vulnerabilities are easier to work with.

 Interested members take leadership roles.

Team members express good ideas, have open discussion, listen without interrupting, and accept insights from others. This is helpful in dealing with conflicting views.

 Team members need a level of comfort before they are able to trust, open up, vent, resolve conflict, and then function effectively.

 The team needs clearly scheduled milestones.

 Face-to-face meetings are needed for confronting difficult issues and reaching closure.

 The free flow of ideas eats up a lot of time in meetings.

## Performing Lessons

 Team activity must compete with other high- or higher-priority initiatives, but developing effective teamwork must be seen as a legitimate activity that is essential to good task and organizational performance.

 Leadership is important for continuing focus and progress of the team.

 Fix the problem, not the blame.

 A team leader is essential.

 Team-building is required before the team can be effective.

 Teams can get a lot done when they are out-to-lunch—team development and team learning often don't happen in a formal meeting.

Team efforts are an investment in the organization's future in multiple ways (e.g., solving problems and increasing networking for information sharing, skill building, leveraging experience, and wise use of people's time and energy).

 A person can work on only so many teams at once.

 The basis for team performance is the recognition of interdependence; we need each other to accomplish what has to be done.

 Collaboration takes a lot of time.

 Communication must be constant.

 Information lives in lots of places one wouldn't expect—inside and outside of commonly held paradigms.

 Teams work if members are committed.

 Commitment leads to passion for the team effort; lack of passion creates a vacuum.

 Delegation allows implementation, but at the cost of control of the outcome.

 To achieve delivery and product integrity, the team must sacrifice. There is never enough time, but the sacrifice must be in proportion to the size of the problem.

 Team learning comes from experience.

Allocate time for forming, storming, norming, and performing every time the team meets, or pay the price of decreased effectiveness later.

 Team members need training on how to become a high-performing team before they can function as one.

 A team can come to consensus, but may wander in the process.

# $\mathcal{F}$OR LEADERS

## Show Up

 Leadership can be distributed and shared. In a word, it rotates.

 Leaders are necessary to team process. Designating a leader is important when responsibility for action must be fixed.

 There are multiple components of leadership. A leader must pay attention to administrative details, must maintain a team focus while being open and inclusive, and must be accountable.

 Leadership can be learned. However, it's hard to do because you can't practice in the basement. You have to do it right in front of the people you want to lead.

## Be Attentive

 Leaders find that emotion and action are inextricably linked. The passion of commitment is both exhilarating and draining.

Leaders set clear objectives and milestones.

 Leaders focus on the task and include everyone involved in the task.

 A leader's expectation of how another should act affects how the leader treats that person.

 Leaders ensure focus in the process and bring closure when necessary, allowing reasonable digressions.

 Leaders encourage an appropriate level of participation.

 Good leaders don't necessarily make good members— they have to learn to be members.

 Leadership is a skill that needs to be practiced.

## Tell the Truth

 Leaders must tell the truth as they see it—and then be open for different viewpoints.

 Leaders focus on excellence.

 Leaders challenge the status quo.

 Leaders need to be sensitive to team members' need for feedback, communicating frequently.

 Leaders create an atmosphere of trust.

Leaders create an environment for learning.

 Leaders deal with different people differently, drawing on the value individuals add, not the differences in personality, behaviors, or experience.

 Establishing a leader among a peer group is difficult and awkward.

## Be Open to Outcomes

 Leaders develop common visions and commitment to the visions by involving those people who work with and around them.

 Leaders stimulate the free flow of ideas.

 Leaders foster nonthreatening environments where learning and leadership take place.

 Leaders are open and inclusive and don't need to run the show.

 Leaders look for common ground before trying to resolve differences.

# Book III

# *A* Guide to
   Team Learning

# *H*OW TO USE
## THIS SECTION

TALENTED TEAMS ARE MADE UP of talented people. But a group does not necessarily make a team. To transform a group into an effective team, the players contribute their own talents as team members, and individual members develop the capacity to act and learn together. Learning is the essential ingredient in working effectively over time. The following models and tools are provided to help individuals be attentive to their own learnings, to apply them to the team, and to aid the team members in learning together.

As individual team members learn to learn together, they are able to apply their learnings with greater finesse, working toward higher productivity. Learning has no beginning or end, but forms a continuous cycle. Therefore, the models and tools are not to be read once and put aside, but revisited frequently. We do not intend that team leaders and members will read this section from cover to cover. Rather, one should be familiar with the contents and the context in which skills may be used. A Tale of Teamwork and Continuous Learning (earlier in this book) which describes the people and events at a fictional company named Fulcrum, provides an example of such context. When team learning or progress is at an impasse, this guide will provide useful suggestions to move the team along to a higher stage of development and productivity. As with all skills, these must be practiced in order to become part of a repertoire of learning activities.

Why are these particular practices important? The leadership required for team learning is based on different concepts from the command and control leadership model of traditional hierarchies. Team leadership and team process are based on commitment generated from common values, common goals, common respect, and a passion for one's work. In a team environment, each member's input can make or break the results. This distinction separates true high-performing teams from their related entities, working groups. Not every task requires a team, to be sure. However, for those tasks dependent on true team effort, the results will be improved by attention to team process.

The suggested tools for team learning, as well as the story of Fulcrum, are based on organizing models of team development and team learning. The purpose for these models is to promote understanding of, as well as to establish expectations for, what is happening as groups of individuals make the transition from groups to teams. The model described by the Four Principles (page 91) applies at each stage of team development, although the expected advantage for using the behavioral tools may differ according to the maturity of the team. The following tools are described through their *purpose, use, benefits,* and *pitfalls* so that the readers can choose the most appropriate practice. To add life to the models and tools, each contains a reference to the fictional learning team at Fulcrum, indicating where the team used the particular tool or might have had smoother sailing if they had chosen to use it. Introducing the behavioral tools for team learning is a Problem Matrix (page 88). The matrix reflects typical problems that teams encounter as they develop and learn together, and it suggests which behavioral tools apply in solving the problem. The matrix is not meant to be all-inclusive; it provides a starting point for using these tools.

# $T$HE VIMA MODEL OF TEAM DEVELOPMENT

| | |
|---|---|
| **Purpose** | This model of team development assists in understanding the process of being a team and in being intentional about the process in order to |

work toward a level of trust, empowerment, and high performance. The model is used both as a mental aid and as a teaching vehicle whenever intentionality and understanding of the team development process can assist in achieving the team's goal.

| | |
|---|---|
| **How to Use This Tool** | Any team member who is versed in the model for team development can help the rest of the team understand where they are in the model. |

By recognizing the stage and its related behaviors, the turmoil related to team development becomes visible and negotiable, rather than a roadblock to further productivity. By using Informal Process Checks (page 108) when taking a time-out to look at team development, a team can learn to assess its own learning.

| | |
|---|---|
| **Benefits** | Development will take place whether one is conscious of it or not. The story of Fulcrum demonstrates that intentionality helps in two ways. |

First, it helps individual team members understand what is happening to them *as it happens*. This knowledge can generate the energy necessary to stay the course in early rough going. Second, it aids understanding of process learnings so the team improves its performance over time, repeating helpful behaviors and avoiding roadblocks.

| **Pitfalls** |
|---|

Models reduce complexity to simplicity. One might assume from the description that the task of becoming a team is simple. Unfortunately, that is not the case. At the same time, overemphasis on the model should not detract from concentration on the team's task. To avoid this pitfall, remember that team development takes time and patience and is done while the team works on its task.

| **Story Application** |
|---|

As the team receives its charge from Gary and begins its formation, it is clear that only Andy has any knowledge of team development as a process (page 10).

> ". . . Teams typically go through stages of development . . . members are asking themselves questions about the cost of membership and whether they will be accepted."

Andy chooses to describe what is happening to the team at the moment with respect to relationships, rather than describe the entire theory. This choice is more palatable to his audience and more practical. Andy tries to pull the group into becoming a team. Often, the pulling is a slow and painful process, but one person with appropriate process skills can make a tremendous difference in team performance.

The VIMA model of team development shows within the triangle what must be accomplished if a group is to become a team. The upward rising arm on the right depicts members' psychological state in the process. The upward rising arm on the left shows the stages of development that will be taking place. Finally, the model indicates the stages at which necessary qualities like trust and empowerment are likely to be developed.

## The Model

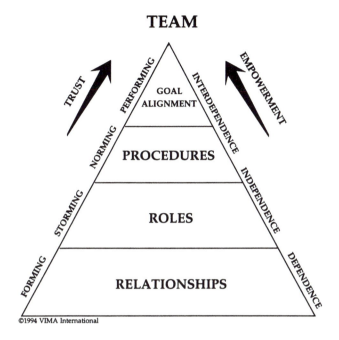

TEAM

©1994 VIMA International

# THE TUCKMAN MODEL OF DEVELOPMENT

| Purpose |
|---------|

The Tuckman model helps team members and leaders understand how small groups work together. Whenever small groups work together, the model applies and can be used to facilitate their team development process.

| How to Use This Tool |
|----------------------|

All team members can use this tool by recognizing that groups are merely numbers of people brought together for a purpose. These people do not necessarily share the same history, assumptions, goals, or values. To become a team, groups must spend time forming, storming, and norming before performing. Patience with the process is a key to using this knowledge to the team's advantage.

| Benefits |
|----------|

Understanding the stages of development allows leaders or team members to effectively intervene to facilitate the progress of their development and performance. An atmosphere of trust can be achieved sooner if the members share assumptions, concerns, and expectations about the team.

---

Tuckman, B. W. (1965). Development sequence in small groups. *Psychological Bulletin,* Vol. 63, pp. 384–399. Used with permission.

| Pitfalls | Becoming enamored with process over task may destroy the balance essential for effective teams. |

To avoid this pitfall and to maintain balance, continually ask these questions:

- Is the team focused on the goal for which we were formed?
- What is happening as we interact with one another?

| Story Application | Andy begins his process instruction to the team with this model (page 10). By being ex- |

plicit about the stages of development, he helps shape the expectations of the other team members about what did and did not constitute success. Pat, however, demonstrates how a misunderstanding of the model can hurt performance more than it helps (page 44).

> "Well, I let them engage in small talk for almost five minutes. Then I cut it off and was the storm myself for a while. When I finished storming, I told them their norm was to go and perform."

Pat errs on the side of overemphasis on the task, giving merely lip service to the process of team development.

## The Model

In the development of any team, certain stages of behavior impact how well the individuals and the team accomplish their task. The five progressive stages in the Tuckman model are:

1. Forming
2. Storming
3. Norming
4. Performing
5. Adjourning

These stages are sequential, and development issues during each stage must be satisfactorily resolved in order for the team to move to the next stage. Unfortunately, resolving the behavioral issues in each stage does not preclude the team from reverting to a *previous* level of development during the life of the team. In fact, each time the team meets or when new members join or former members leave, the formation process begins again.

Whenever teams work together, an emphasis on getting the job done can deter their effectiveness if attention is not also directed to the relationship issues in the development stages, as well as to the task at hand. As members understand the relationship issues and the psychological state in each stage (see Table 1), it becomes easier to move on to productive performance. Although the team may revert to previous stages with lapses in time and changes in membership, it may move more quickly through subsequent stages with individual and team maturity, understanding of task complexity, effective leadership, and positive organizational climate.

**TABLE 1**
**Tuckman's Summary of Sequential Development in Teams**

| Stages of Team Development | Task Behavior | Relationship Behavior | Psychological State |
|---|---|---|---|
| 1. Forming | Orientation | Testing and dependence | Dependence |
| 2. Storming | Emotional response to task demands | Intragroup hostility | Independence |
| 3. Norming | Expression of opinions | Development of team cohesion | Interdependence |
| 4. Performing | Emergence of solutions | Functional role-relatedness | Interdependence |
| 5. Adjourning | Termination | Disengagement | Grief |

# Stages of Team Development

## Stage I: Forming

Team members discover what behaviors are acceptable to others. For newly established teams, this stage is the transition from individual to member status. For teams with new leadership, mission, or members, this stage is a period of testing behavior. In either situation, the psychological state is dependence.

*Characteristics:*

- Members attempt to identify tasks in terms of relevant parameters and to decide how the team will accomplish the tasks.

- Members exhibit hesitant participation or low involvement. Feelings are neither identified nor dealt with. Weaknesses are covered up. Members do not want to rock the boat.

- Intellectualizing—an attitude of "the workplace is for work"—prevails. Members' expectations follow established lines of authority.

- Complaints about the organizational environment, such as unclear objectives or poor listening, prevail.

- Suspicion, fear, and anxiety about the new situation in light of other more pressing requirements are common.

- Minimal work is accomplished relative to the capabilities of the individual members.

## Stage II: Storming

Team members express their individuality and resist team formation.

*Characteristics:*

- Infighting, defensiveness, competition, jealousy, and increased tension abound.

- Resistance occurs because the task demands are perceived to interfere with personal or other organizational needs.
- Polarization of members is demonstrated by the raising and debating of risky issues.
- Concern arises over excessive work as the team considers wider options.
- Some individual members begin to raise personal feelings; others listen more.
- Pecking orders are established as the team agrees to some task assignments.
- Minimal work is accomplished relative to the capabilities of the individual members.

## Stage III: Norming

Members accept the team, the team norms, their own roles, and the idiosyncrasies of other members.

*Characteristics:*

- An atmosphere of trust develops.
- A high level of intimacy is characterized by team members' confiding in each other, sharing personal problems, and discussing team dynamics.
- A new ability to express emotions constructively is evidenced.
- A sense of team cohesiveness accompanies a common spirit and goals.
- The establishment and maintenance of team boundaries takes place.
- Moderate work is accomplished relative to the capabilities of the individual members.

## Stage IV: Performing

The team becomes an entity capable of diagnosing and solving problems and making decisions. Stage IV is not always reached by groups, but is the distinguishing difference between groups and teams.

*Characteristics:*

- Members experience insight into personal and interpersonal processes.
- High flexibility, appropriate leadership, maximum use of resources, and recognition of personal obligations are common.
- Constructive self-change is undertaken as self-development becomes a team priority.
- More work is accomplished than could be anticipated, given the capabilities of individual members.

### Stage V: Adjourning

This final stage brings the team to an end.

*Characteristics:*

- Task behaviors are terminated and relationships are disengaged.
- When planned, members say personal good-byes and recognize each other's participation and accomplishments.

As teams progress through the forming, storming, norming, and performing stages, both the level of trust and the degree of empowerment increase. Only by diligently working through the process issues of relationships, roles, procedures, and goal alignment can a group become a team and be truly high performing.

# *L*IGHT BULBS FOR LEADERS PROBLEM MATRIX

INDIVIDUALS OFTEN EXPERIENCE particular problems when working in teams. One is often asked, "How do you handle the situation when . . . ." There is never an easy answer to this question. The most accurate answer is, "It depends on the situation." This response is never helpful to a person who is feeling the frustration of trying unsuccessfully to have a group of individuals work together as a team. The matrix that follows is an attempt to provide greater structure or guidance for the answer.

| **Purpose** | The Problem Matrix is designed to be a starting place in considering which tools apply to typical issues or problems that arise in groups that |

are developing into teams. Successfully working through these problems is critical to achieving progress in the process and to accomplishing synergistic teamwork.

| **How to Use This Tool** | Think about the problem you perceive with your group or team. Examine the left-hand column of the matrix with your problem in |

mind, and try to find a similar problem. Then look to the body of the matrix to find a bullet under a suggested tool. At this point,

## TABLE 2
## Light Bulbs for Leaders Problem Matrix

| Page numbers | Meeting Checklist 96 | EIAG 98 | Listening With Empathy 104 | Meeting Communications Check 106 | Informal Process Checks 108 | Assessing Team Behavior 111 | Leader Effectiveness Check 118 | Team Effectiveness Check 119 | Meeting Process Check 120 | Feedback: Giving and Receiving 121 | Stop/Start/Continue 128 | Asking Open Questions 131 | Learning Through Dialogue 134 |
|---|---|---|---|---|---|---|---|---|---|---|---|---|---|
| Turf Battles | • | | | | | | | | | | | | |
| When no one is in charge | | • | | | • | • | | | | • | | • | • |
| Getting off the subject | | | • | | | | • | • | | | | | |
| Not sharing information | | | | • | • | • | | • | • | • | | • | |
| Not working synergistically in teams | | • | | • | • | • | | • | | | | | • |
| Team not making progress | | | • | • | • | • | • | • | | | • | • | • |
| Conflicting goals and priorities | | | | | • | | | • | | | • | | • |
| Lack of attendance | • | • | • | | | • | | • | | • | | | |
| People late to meetings | • | • | | | | | | | | • | | | |
| Hidden agendas | | | • | • | • | | • | • | • | • | • | | |
| Mental roadblocks | | | | | • | • | | | | • | | • | • |
| Group membership—who's in or out? | • | • | | | | | | | • | | | | • |
| Heightened emotions | | | | | • | • | | | | • | | | |
| Not listening | | | • | • | | | • | • | • | | | • | |
| Nay saying | | | • | • | | | • | • | • | | | | |
| Cynicism | | | | • | | • | | | • | | • | | |
| Follow-up | | | | | | | • | • | • | | • | | • |

exercise great caution. Which tool to select is a value judgment on the part of the selector. Your choice should be based on the situation, your comfort with using the tool, and the expected reaction of other group or team members.

| Benefits | Careful use of this Problem Matrix will assist in identifying the correct processes to use in becoming a high performance team. |

| Pitfalls | The danger is that the matrix can become an end in itself. To avoid this pitfall, keep in mind that it is only a beginning point. The real work of process intervention takes place after the tool is selected. |

| Story Application | The team at Fulcrum did not have the Problem Matrix at its disposal. On the other hand, it did have one member with some process skills. In the beginning, the group depended on Andy almost exclusively for its attention to process. Later, each member was free to intervene as necessary. This should be the case for your application. Use the Problem Matrix with discipline at first. Later, let go of dependence on it. (See Table 2.) |

# $\mathcal{F}$OUR PRINCIPLES OF LEADERSHIP

| | |
|---|---|
| **Purpose** | This model applies to both leadership and life situations. Furthermore, it represents an easy-to-remember set of requirements that is useful |

in each of the five stages of team development. The model frames one's thinking about the impact of one's behavior on others. That is, it provides an answer to the question: What can I do to improve this situation?

| | |
|---|---|
| **How to Use This Tool** | As requirements for learning, the four principles are available both consciously and unconsciously to all team members. Each individual |

can use the principles as a guide to individual behavior and to interpersonal behavior. By asking oneself or others the questions implied by each principle, team members are able to be in consonance with their own values, assumptions, and goals in working toward accomplishing the goal of the team.

1. Do I show up mentally and physically?
2. Am I attentive to what has heart and meaning?

---

Arrien, A. (1993). *The four-fold way,* (pp. 7–8) San Francisco: Harper Collins Publishers. Used with permission.

3. Do I tell the truth without blame or judgment?

4. Am I open to outcomes other than my own?

**Benefits**  The principles of leadership help to frame events so one can learn from them and transfer the learnings to other situations. The principles also assist in improving performance in the current setting.

**Pitfalls**  The principles could become yet one more category used to criticize others who are less skilled in their struggle to influence others. To avoid this pitfall, concentrate on the principle that suggests "without blame or judgment."

**Story Application**  These principles appear late in the story. Andy, true to the principle of continuous learning, and caring about the development of others on his high-performance team, shared his learning with Pat. Pat relayed this information to Janet on the phone (page 52).

> "He says there are four requirements. The first is to *show up*. In essence, you have to be there to influence what's going on. Then, to lead, you have to *be attentive*—that is, pay attention to what people are doing. Learn what has heart and meaning for those you're trying to influence. Next, the leader has to *tell the truth without blame or judgment*. Finally, one has to be *open to outcomes*."

A careful reading of the model shows that Pat missed some fine points, and, in subsequent conversation with Janet, he showed that his superficial understanding has led to dismissal of the whole concept. Thankfully, Janet was more persistent as she and Pat struggled to apply their learnings.

## The Principles

From the earliest times, societies have acknowledged four guiding principles that create balance in the life of an individual and a

community. These principles are widely applicable. '
plied to teamwork, the four principles organize one'
about appropriate process interventions that can tr
group of individuals into a learning team. These fou
are the organizing model for the tools presented in th

## I. Show Up and Choose to Be Present

One must be present both physically and mentally in order to influence others. Influencing others and being influenced by them
require that each individual on a team be present in body and
mind.

## II. Be Attentive to What Has Heart and Meaning

This principle is a listening requirement. One must listen simultaneously to oneself and to others. That requires an answer to the
question: What is one feeling at this moment? What is the mood
of others? How are the words that are being said and not said im-
pacting this situation?

## III. Tell the Truth without Blame or Judgment

This principle gives voice to the feelings being experienced as one
listens. Without voice, learning cannot take place, teams cannot
develop synergy, and individuals remain stuck in the phase that
is giving the team difficulty. As one gives voice to these feelings,
it is important to own them as one's own, not to project them on
others with blame or judgment.

## IV. Be Open to Outcomes, Not Attached to Outcomes

One who has chosen to show up does so with a particular goal in
mind. It is critical for each team member to remain open to accept
others' stated or implied goals. Without such openness, individuals may fight and even win, but the team and organization will be
the ultimate losers.

# $P$RINCIPLE ONE: SHOW UP

80 percent of living is simply showing up.

—Woody Allen

WOODY ALLEN IS SURELY CORRECT in the context of the principles of leadership. If one fails to show up physically or mentally, none of the other principles can come into play. With respect to the team of directors from Fulcrum, there are numerous examples of both showing up and failing to do so. The principle is of particular importance in the forming stage of team development. Janice identifies the problem early, when she questions Andy about John's absence (page 12).

> "Sure," said Janice, "but I think you're forgetting something that may be important. If I understand this forming stage, it's where boundaries get formed. In other words, we know by the boundaries who's in and who's out, right?"
> Andy smiled, "That's great, Janice; yet another learning."
> "Well," Janice responded, pleased with her correctness, "what about John? Is he or is he not a part of this team?"

Successfully working through this issue of absence contributed to the establishment of a team norm about how to handle other absences more successfully in future meetings. Moreover, it surfaced the requirement that leadership within the team is contingent on showing up. If one is not present, one's influence is lost.

Supporting the principle of showing up are two behavioral tools to promote team learning. The Meeting Checklist (page 97) helps the designated leader to prepare in advance and to facilitate the preparation of other team members. It is general in nature and will surely need to be adapted to particular situations. The EIAG (page 98) is a method to focus thinking and behavior in order to ensure that team members attend to and learn from process outcomes of the team's activities and development.

## Meeting Checklist

| Purpose |
| --- |

To ensure proper preparation for team gatherings, necessary assignments are made for content and process needs during the meeting, and for follow-up after the meeting. When used routinely, the meeting checklist ensures that needs unmet in the meeting do not destroy the productivity of the team.

| How to Use This Tool |
| --- |

The person who is responsible for meeting logistics can use this checklist to ensure that significant arrangements have been made for the meeting. It includes assignment of actions to be done before, during, and after the meeting (see Table 3, page 97).

| Benefits |
| --- |

The Meeting Checklist provides a structure that gives team members comfort in the early stages of team development and helps to build and reinforce trust during later stages. It allows for a smooth meeting— one in which logistical and process needs are met and decisions are not left hanging.

| Pitfalls |
| --- |

Slavish adherence to any standard structure or procedure can become a hindrance to team learning. To avoid this pitfall, the person responsible for scheduling or conducting the meeting should consciously modify the checklist requirements to meet the needs of the particular situation.

## TABLE 3
### Meeting Checklist

| | *Before* |
|---|---|
| Objective | What do I want to achieve by the end of the meeting? Is a meeting the best way to handle this? |
| People who should attend | Who needs the information? Who can contribute? Who would expect to be involved? |
| Amount of prior notice | How long do people need to prepare? What information needs to be assembled? |
| Agenda | Items from previous meetings New items How much time will be needed? Ending time |
| Background information | What information can be supplied in advance? |
| Prework | What should participants prepare before they come? |
| Room | What seating is needed? Which room should be booked? What equipment is needed? |
| | *During* |
| Notes | Who will take notes? |
| Breaks | Will breaks be needed? |
| Process | How will the attendees be intentional about process? (See Informal Process Checks, page 108 and Assessing Team Behavior, page 111) |
| | *After* |
| Record | Will minutes be published? Will they show who is to take action and by when? When will they go out? |

**Story Application** No specific instance of using this tool is evident in the story. However, without specific mention of it, the team recognized to some extent the necessity for structure (page 5).

"We have to put an end time on the meeting because I have to co-ordinate child care with my wife," said Andy. The five agreed on a 5:00 P.M. stop time and found a day the next week when it was possible to meet. John agreed to tell Pat of the plans.

One might imagine that its more deliberate use, especially in the first two meetings, would have resulted in smoother progress for the team (page 27).

"We didn't appoint a leader for this session," exclaimed Pat, slapping his forehead. "This team stuff isn't so hard, we just keep forgetting our past learnings. Whose fault is that?" "Fixing the blame doesn't help us make progress. . . ."

As the characters learned, any process tool such as this meeting checklist should be used specifically to contribute to team learning and performance, not to place blame for omissions.

## EIAG: Experience, Identify, Analyze, Generalize

| Purpose |

The four steps—*experience, identify, analyze,* and *generalize*—help individuals and teams elicit learnings from their experience. These four steps may be applied to any event that has just happened. They assess individual learning, team dynamics, and team development. By generalizing the learnings, teams know what actions to replicate and what actions to avoid in order to achieve continuous learning.

| How to Use This Tool |

The EIAG process is a deliberate consideration by the participants of any activity (experience) that has been shared. Participants consciously discuss each of the steps. Following the experience, participants

---

Rubin, I., Kolb, D., Osland, J. M. (1979). *Organizational behavior: An experiential approach.* Englewood Cliffs, NJ: Prentice-Hall. Used with permission.

identify exactly what happened behaviorally. They then analyze what those behaviors meant for them, how they felt about them, and how the behaviors helped or hindered progress toward the goal. From that analysis, the team generalizes learnings that they will practice during their next team activity.

| Benefits |

The model is easy to apply to maximize learning from any experience. It allows teams to continuously improve based on their own experiences and to perform after-action reviews on their own performance before it becomes a problem.

| Pitfalls |

The intervention may become an end in itself rather than a means to facilitate learning. To avoid this pitfall, teams must actively focus on the goal of their task. After working on the task, the team spends a shorter amount of time on the EIAG and sets process goals for the next experience together.

| Story Application |

In essence, each time the characters list learnings, they have articulated them by having an experience, identifying what happened, analyzing the event, and generalizing from it. John demonstrates this clearly (page 18).

"I agree." Now it was John's turn. "I don't think we've avoided anything, Andy. Record as a process learning that in effective teams, leadership rotates. The person who has the most passion about a particular topic will jump up and grab the pen and take charge. That's what's been happening here, and we are feeling great about what we've done."

## EIAG: Four Steps

1. Experience. Do something (create an experience) as a team. After the experience ends, continue with the next three steps. Reflection on the value of the experience may

take place in a feedback session, in after-action team critiques, or after planned experiential learning events.

2. Identify. Consider the experience, and describe specifically what happened. What action, activity, or behavior has been identified from the experience? What was the sequence of events? Who did what, and when?

3. Analyze. What were the team members thinking about during the experience? What were they feeling? Make observations or draw conclusions about the nature of what happened. How were the events and behaviors related to people's thoughts and feelings? How did the actions impact others? Was the team's performance or progress on the task affected? What helped, and what got in the way of progress?

4. Generalize. What general learnings are implied from the discussion? Generate guidelines for how to handle similar situations in the future. What might be done differently or the same? What advice would be given? Document the answers as learnings from this experience. When the team meets again, reiterate those learnings, and consciously practice behaviors based on those learnings in order to improve performance.

### EIAG: An Example

Consider a situation in which an ongoing team experiences a change in membership. This event takes the team back to the forming stage of team development. To facilitate learning and progression through the stages, an EIAG can reveal underlying roadblocks to team development and progress on the task. The EIAG can be facilitated by an external process facilitator or by an appointed member of the team who has appropriate skills. Given this particular example, the EIAG might address the following questions in an effort to assess the change in the team dynamics:

- What happened to our team when membership changed?
- What processes did we experience that were different from the previous membership?
- Why did we experience those differences?
- What did we appreciate about our original team?
- What bothered us about our original team?
- What do we appreciate about our new team?
- Who participates in the team discussion and what is each participant's role?
- Who does not participate in the team discussion and with what effect?
- Based on this discussion, how would we behave differently next time to include the new member?

*Warning:* If you focus too intently on the questions themselves, you may destroy the positive team dynamic you're trying to create. Remember, the EIAG is a means to improve team learning, not an end in itself!

# PRINCIPLE TWO: BE ATTENTIVE

**We have two ears and only one tongue in order that we may hear more and speak less.**

**—Diogenes**

THE ESSENCE OF THIS PRINCIPLE is to pay attention to what has heart and meaning for oneself and for others. Teams cannot reach a state of interdependence unless members are in tune with each other and can anticipate each other's moods, reactions, and feelings.

George, Janice's deputy, epitomizes this principle at the end of the meeting with her 20 subordinates. The chapter opens with George making a lucky guess about his boss needing a cup of coffee (page 45).

> ". . . our secretary said you were speaking with Pat on the phone. He can be a pain sometimes, so I got the coffee. . . ."

For the next two pages, he listens to her speak about her concerns in reference to the just-concluded meeting. He responds to each of these concerns with thoughtful and honest reactions. Toward the end of the section, he reveals his own anxiety about the project he has volunteered to lead (page 47).

". . . Is that the only reason you wanted to talk?"

"Not really. I was hoping for some more guidance about the video teleconference tomorrow."

George's comments reveal that he is being attentive to Janice and her situation at the same time that he is in touch with his own needs. It is clear that each person needs the other. The boss needs positive feedback on her actions. The subordinate needs guidance, or at least reassurance, on a tough project. In a real sense, this professional colleague relationship represents the ideal to strive for. Perhaps it is an ideal because one so rarely finds such a relationship within an organization.

This section contains four tools to help one be more attentive. None of the tools, in and of themselves, will cause a person to attend to self or to others. However, when applied as techniques to increase awareness, they can contribute measurably to the state of interdependence as the team develops.

## Listening with Empathy

**Purpose**

Communication requires a constant negotiation for meaning, which is defined by the listener. To listen with empathy is the first step in the development of meaning. To clarify the meaning requires one to hear and understand what another person is saying through words, tone, and body language.

**How to Use This Tool**

This tool requires both self-discipline and restraint. One must discipline oneself to actually listen, while restraining the natural urge to interject one's reaction to what is being said. The listener must consciously accept words, tone, and body language in order to consider the speaker's experiences, assumptions, values, and suggestions.

| Benefits | Listening with empathy benefits both the speaker and the listener by encouraging genuineness, acceptance, and respect. This attention increases |

trust within the team.

| Pitfalls | Listening with empathy is a difficult task for most people. It requires commitment, skill, and practice, as well as the need to suspend judg- |

ment. To overcome this pitfall, one must frequently practice the range of effective listening skills.

| Story Application | Janice indicates her ability to listen to others as she describes her encounter on the freeway (page 24). |

"... I stood back and marveled at how none of those individuals would listen to the others. ..."

She could listen and understand what the problem was, but was unable to get the others to join her in the listening endeavor.

## Listening Skills

Because listening is something we do every day, we are likely to take the act of listening for granted. Examining the various skills that cluster in three dominant areas—*following*, *attending*, and *reflecting*—helps to refine the act and the art of listening.

## I. Following

Exhibiting listening behaviors that show you are hearing what the person is saying helps focus the speaker's thoughts. These *following* skills are:

1. Providing silence, which creates room for others to speak.
2. Initiating door openers to invite others to speak.

3. Saying "I hear you" responses, which provide reassuring feedback.

4. Asking open-ended questions, which elicit information from the speaker (page 131).

## II. Attending

To show that you are paying attention to what the person is saying, the skills in *attending* are:

1. Choosing posture that demonstrates active awareness of the speaker and her or his position.
2. Making eye contact with the speaker.
3. Making gestures to recognize the content and style of the speaker's words.
4. Creating an environment that is conducive to hearing.

## III. Reflecting

These skills illustrate that you, the listener, are clearly seeking to understand what is being said. These *reflecting* skills are:

1. Paraphrasing the content of the speaker's message.
2. Reflecting both the content of the message and the feelings you interpret from the speaker.
3. Summarizing what you have heard.
4. Clarifying your understanding of the meaning of the message.

A conscious effort to use these skills will enhance the quality of communication and highlight the real meaning of the exchange.

## Meeting Communication Check

| Purpose |

Paying attention to communication patterns during meetings allows the team to understand how well it is working together. Data about communication patterns are required to begin any team discussion that could improve communication and advance team development. The Meeting Communication Check assists in objectivity and can be applied to any team meeting.

| **How to Use This Tool** | Initially, this tool should be used quietly and individually, in writing. Record the answers to the Meeting Communication Check questions |

on a piece of paper. If the results seem stark or surprising enough, one option is to publish the results among the team and discuss the implications. This discussion can be moderated by a process facilitator or a team member who is skilled in observation and feedback.

| **Benefits** | Objective data assist in attending to the dynamics of meetings—morale, influence, communication, participation, conflict, competition, and |

cooperation—and enable early diagnosis of meeting problems in order to deal with them more effectively.

| **Pitfalls** | Having gathered such data, one may draw erroneous conclusions about the data. To avoid this pitfall, one must be open to outcomes in discuss- |

ing the meaning of the team's communication patterns and the potential implications for team effectiveness.

| **Story Application** | Although not explicitly stated, it is apparent that this type of data is being gathered by the entire team (page 24). |

When the team reassembled, Pat asked to take the lead in explaining what had transpired in Janice's absence. His stepping forward pleased the others, because he had been fairly silent during the proceedings. He explained to Janice that Lois and Andy had started storming on the technology-versus-people issue, and that John had done a masterful job of summarizing their respective points and getting each to listen to the others. "I assigned myself the role of making sure the comments you and Ted made last night, as well as my own thinking, were well represented," he concluded. . . ."

Pat's synopsis to the team reflected their communication patterns, the understanding of which contributed to productive and synergistic results.

## The Communication Check

Answers to the questions in the Meeting Communication Check will reveal whether the participation is balanced among members. Consider the following questions to determine the level of communication:

- Who talks to whom?
- Who interrupts whom?
- Who talks, dominates, or withdraws?

From your answers, consider whether the communication flow helps or hinders full participation. Refer to the information on Assessing Team Behavior (page 111) to evaluate the performance of the team. Count, in a given time period during the session:

- Number of interruptions;
- Number of suggestions or proposals not responded to;
- How often the team reverts to a win/lose majority vote versus working toward a consensus. (What circumstances seem to drive the team toward a win/lose vote?).

From your answers, determine the level of involvement and participation among team members. Decide whether your assumptions should be discussed with the team as a way of increasing team development and productivity.

## Informal Process Checks

| Purpose |

An Informal Process Check is an intervention, during a team meeting or interpersonal exchange, designed to assess what is actually going on and whether it is helpful to the goal of the team's activity. It may be used when any individual thinks the task or process of the exchange is off-track and the team needs to be redirected.

| **How to Use This Tool** | Whenever you are thinking one thought but saying something else or nothing at all, consider interrupting the team to ask others |

whether they sense a roadblock or less-than-open communication.

| **Benefits** | The use of process checks enables the team to keep a constant focus on improving their process. |

| **Pitfalls** | Process checks may be perceived as interruptive and intrusive. To avoid this pitfall, do not overuse the intervention, and ask for permission to stop |

the team process to do a check.

| **Story Application** | Andy instructs the team on the use of process checks (page 11). |

"We use a technique called *process checks* We stop the content discussion and check out with one another what is really going on. We examine the process we are using to see whether it is helping us or getting in the way of our achieving the goal. For example, when we have a discussion and hidden agendas get in the way, we say things that we don't really mean . . . ."

Later, Ted tries Andy's suggestion. He uses the following approach (page 15).

"In answer to your question, Pat, I don't know 'what,'" returned Ted. "I've been trying to figure out why my gut feel doesn't match what we're all doing right now, as Andy suggested, and I can't put my finger on it. But I still had to say something. I have a sinking feeling we're getting nowhere fast. Do you have any ideas, Andy?"

Ted's reflection of what he was feeling served as a process check to address a roadblock in the team's progress.

# Process Checks

Informal process checks are powerful and effective interventions that any person may use when the process seems to be off-track. Process checks are instant and easy, providing immediate feedback and course correction for individual and team performance.

The need for a process check may be obvious or may be a gut feeling. Indicators that a process check is in order may be the feeling that the team has lost focus, that participation is uneven, that hidden agendas are being played out, that power plays are hindering open discussion, or that other dysfunctional behaviors are occurring.

Whenever one is thinking one thought but saying something else or not saying anything at all, one should consider using a process check. What one is thinking internally and not saying is probably authentic and often reflects what other people are thinking and feeling but not saying. Using a process check allows all members of the discussion to consider where the discussion is going and to make an effort to come back to open, honest dialogue in working toward a goal.

Any member of the discussion can ask for a process check. Simply enter the discussion by requesting time for a process check. Then ask an appropriate question, such as one of these:

- What's happening in the team right now?
- Are we addressing the issue at hand?
- Are there concerns that are not being expressed?
- Do we need to refocus on the agenda?

If the question does not provoke a process examination, a feeling statement might be in order, such as:

- I'm feeling frustrated that we have lost focus in our discussion.
- I wonder if we're storming rather than discussing the topic.

- I'm concerned that we're not hearing input from all the members present.
- I'm afraid that other issues or individual concerns are hampering our progress. Does anyone else feel that way?

When the process questions have been answered satisfactorily, the team can continue working on the task with more productive discussion.

## Assessing Team Behavior

**Purpose**

Recognizing functional as well as dysfunctional behaviors helps to clarify how a team is performing. This allows team members to improve the working climate and interpersonal relationships. Sharpening one's observation of team behavior helps to move the team forward in its development.

**How to Use This Tool**

The team should discuss the functional and dysfunctional behaviors of task and maintenance team dynamics in order to agree on what is acceptable for the team in meeting its goal. Team members can agree ahead of time to call an Informal Process Check (page 108) when behavior begins to impede the team's progress.

**Benefits**

Sharing a clarity of definitions for functional as well as dysfunctional behaviors will increase one's astuteness in observing team behavior. Sharing observations leads to openness and increases trust.

**Pitfalls**

Team behavior is not easy to define or detect. It is difficult to share negative assessments in a constructive way. To overcome this pitfall, a team discussion of behavioral norms should take place before behavior becomes dysfunctional. A process facilitator is helpful in bringing out dysfunctional assessments in a nondefensive way.

| Story Application | The story provides several examples of team members' assessing their own behavior. In an early example, Andy comments (page 9).

> "That's one of the observations I have," answered Andy. "The idea of setting an agenda and following it is critical to meeting management and also raises the question of team leader. Who's in charge of this team anyway? And since no one paid attention to Lois's earlier comment about her agenda, have we just wasted three hours of our meeting time?"

Seldom does anyone come to work planning to throw a monkey wrench into the day's proceedings. Yet, some circumstances can cause behavior to occur that is not helpful to the individual or to the team. Understanding the signs of certain behaviors, both functional and dysfunctional, allows the team to become more effective. The following descriptions will sharpen awareness of what is really happening.

### Functional Behaviors

Maintenance-oriented behaviors help the team remain in good working order with a positive climate and effective relationships. The behaviors are:

- Participating and including—helping communication remain open; inviting others to participate.
- Supporting and encouraging—using facial expressions and remarks to let others know they have been heard.
- Openness—a willingness to yield when conflict to one's own idea arises; volunteering to modify one's position in order to maintain team cohesiveness; admitting errors.
- Testing agreement/reality—using Informal Process Checks (page 108) to test the team's satisfaction with its procedures; pointing out norms that may need to be tested.

- Harmonizing—encouraging team members to explore difficulties in their relationships.

Task-oriented behaviors help the team's problem solving and improve performance on the task assigned. The behaviors are:

- Initiating procedures—proposing or initiating effective meeting management processes (see the Meeting Checklist, page 97).
- Generating (requesting) information—asking for facts and information as well as for expression of feelings; seeking expression of values and assumptions (see Asking Open Questions, page 131).
- Generating (giving) information—providing facts and suggestions that are useful in accomplishing the team's task at hand; stating a belief about a matter before the team.
- Decision testing—offering to test whether the team is close to a decision; proposing a possible conclusion.
- Problem clarifying—helping to clear up confusion by interpreting input; suggesting alternatives.
- Summarizing—restating the team's discussions; pulling together related ideas.

## Dysfunctional Behaviors

Dysfunctional behaviors interfere with the team's ability to operate as a team in accomplishing the task at hand. These behaviors may be overt and aggressive or covert and passive.

- Blocking—arguing several positions; returning to dead issues; nit-picking.
- Withdrawing—removing oneself from participation mentally and/or physically; repeated side conversations; doing other work.

- Digressing—taking the team down a primrose path of unrelated issues and information; telling war stories.
- Seeking recognition—loud or excessive joking or cheap shots aimed at diverting attention from the task to the jokester; drawing attention from the task to oneself to meet personal needs.
- Interrupting—using irrelevant input to abruptly stop the dialogue or discussion; repeatedly cutting others off in midsentence.
- Hidden agenda—listening for the "yes, but" routine; behaviors designed to manipulate the team's focus onto one's personal agenda, which is never explicitly stated.

# $\mathcal{P}$RINCIPLE THREE: TELL THE TRUTH

**If you wish to astonish the whole world, tell the simple truth.**

—Rahel

ONCE ONE SHOWS UP AND IS ATTENTIVE to what has heart and meaning for oneself and others, the task is to express one's thoughts and feelings in a way that other members of the team can receive and use. This often requires courage, and it always requires discipline. The quote by Rahel suggests that truth-telling is not as natural as one would hope. It is not natural because one person's truth is not necessarily another person's truth.

The team from Fulcrum is engaging in truth-telling (page 17). Andy observes that the team has avoided the leadership issue and has simply been announcing conflicting conclusions. This is the truth for Andy, but not everyone . . .

"I could buy that—if it were true," challenged Pat. "You're obviously leading now and did at the beginning of the meeting, too."

"Yes and no," said Ted. "Andy's leading now and did at the beginning, but I think all the avoidance of the subject came when we were trying to get into the content part of our work. Even if we accept that what he's talking about is important, it's way outside our area of expertise and has little to do with what we tell Gary."

"Why does it have so little to do with what we tell Gary?" This came from Janice who had silently gone halfway through her dinner in deep thought. . . .

As depicted in the VIMA model of team development (page 77), once team members begin to express the truth as they see it, they can develop meaningful norms for procedures that will produce the synergistic results organizations hope for from teams.

This section contains three checklists and a feedback model that are excellent for expressing one's truth. As is true for Principle Two, these tools simply facilitate reaching the end goal of truth-telling. Actually getting there requires discipline and dedication on the part of each individual team member.

## Checklists That Help Build Effective Teams

**Purpose** The three checklists that follow assist team members in examining their effectiveness as a team as well as the effectiveness of the leader. The checklists provide team members clear, objective data on the effectiveness of their process and encourage discussion on how to modify their behavior.

**How to Use This Tool** Initially, it is helpful to conclude each team meeting by asking each member to complete one or two of the three checklists. Choose the Meeting Process Checklist, which is more general and covers both the team and the leader, or choose both the Leader Effectiveness Checklist and the Team Effectiveness Checklist. Once the team begins to mature, the checklists should be modified to meet specific agreed-on goals of the members. The results of individual checklists should be discussed by the team members in order to improve leader, team, and meeting effectiveness for the next team action.

**Benefits** Checking the effectiveness of the team as well as the leader contributes to a balance between content and process by causing the team members to intentionally address process questions in the checklists. This enables individuals to discuss and modify leadership and team behaviors.

| Pitfalls | Considerable time is required to complete and discuss the checklists. Initially, members may not see the value in spending this precious resource. |

Difficulties may arise in a team of peers, as was the situation in the story, or in teams with differing levels of organizational hierarchy. This pitfall can be avoided if members engage in truth-telling as they see it, without blame or judgment, for the benefit of the team.

| Story Application | The team of peers at Fulcrum did not actually use a formal checklist. They relied on the expertise of one member, Andy, to lead their process observations and interventions. |

This approach worked well for them, but these checklists would have enabled the team to work through process interventions more smoothly and intentionally without the aid of an expert.

### What to Do with the Checklists

The Checklists for Meeting Process, Leader Effectiveness, and Team Effectiveness are useful guides in analyzing and discussing the desired behaviors of both team leaders and members. A few items may be selected from each checklist in order to create a more positive impact. The Leader Effectiveness Check may be used for a single leader or for multiple leaders if the leadership of the team rotates.

The checklists should be used openly and frequently as teams begin the process of working together. At the end of each meeting, the teams should allocate time to review the behaviors from the checklist questions. This exercise will remind them of desired behaviors and will analyze their interactions during the team development process. By consciously using these tools early in the process and revisiting them often, the preferred process, leader, and team behaviors will become more familiar to team members. The purposely scheduled discussions will then increase individuals' comfort levels with Assessing Team Behavior (page 111) and performing Informal Process Checks (page 108).

To improve team effectiveness, the members should focus on behaviors causing the greatest interference and behaviors creating the greatest synergy. Identifying both positive and negative behaviors is critical in recognizing successes and in identifying areas that need improvement. To address individual behaviors, refer to the Feedback tool (page 121). Members of the team should emphasize giving to each other feedback that is behavioral, specific, and changeable.

Initially, this discussion may benefit from a process facilitator's guidance. The checklists are designed, however, as a guide to self-discussion. There is no need to collate or tabulate numerical results. Rather, the questions and individual assessments are a starting point for team discussion and Learning through Dialog (page 134) in order to improve team effectiveness.

### Leader Effectiveness Check

Using the scale, rate the assigned leader's actions during a specific team phase.

| 1 | Rarely or never | 2 | Once in a while | 3 | Sometimes |
| 4 | Fairly often | 5 | Very frequently or always | | |

1. The leader embraced the task enthusiastically.  1  2  3  4  5

2. The leader set clear objectives and milestones.  1  2  3  4  5

3. The leader kept all team members informed.  1  2  3  4  5

4. The leader challenged the status quo solution.  1  2  3  4  5

5. The leader asked, "What can we learn?"  1  2  3  4  5

6. The leader communicated a positive outlook.  1  2  3  4  5

7. The leader enlisted a common vision.  1  2  3  4  5

8. The leader involved others in planning.  1  2  3  4  5

9. The leader treated others with respect.  1  2  3  4  5

10. The leader developed cooperative relationships.  1  2  3  4  5

11. The leader created an atmosphere of trust.    1  2  3  4  5

12. The leader practiced what she or he espoused
    ("walked the talk").                          1  2  3  4  5

13. The leader encouraged participation by all
    team members.                                 1  2  3  4  5

14. The leader recognized others' contributions.  1  2  3  4  5

15. The leader held team members accountable.     1  2  3  4  5

16. The leader gave the team appreciation and
    support.                                      1  2  3  4  5

## *Team Effectiveness Check*

Using the scale, rate the team's actions during a specific working session.

| | | |
|---|---|---|
| 1  Rarely or never | 2  Once in a while | 3  Sometimes |
| 4  Fairly often | 5  Very frequently or always | |

1. Members expressed real feelings.               1  2  3  4  5

2. Members openly disagreed with each other
   when they did disagree.                        1  2  3  4  5

3. Members addressed their remarks to each
   other.                                         1  2  3  4  5

4. Members spoke up without asking permission.    1  2  3  4  5

5. Members took turns handling "problem
   members."                                      1  2  3  4  5

6. "Bright ideas" originated with many members
   of the team.                                   1  2  3  4  5

7. Different individuals led the team's thinking,
   discussion, and procedure.                     1  2  3  4  5

8. Members listened to each other without
   interrupting.                                  1  2  3  4  5

9. Conflicts and disagreements arose, but members tried to understand the nature of the problems and to deal with them. 1 2 3 4 5

10. Members sought insights and information from other members. 1 2 3 4 5

11. Members accepted insights and information from other members. 1 2 3 4 5

12. Members drew out and questioned each other to better understand their contributions. 1 2 3 4 5

13. When a problem-solving meeting was finished, all the members of the team understood and supported the decision reached. 1 2 3 4 5

## Meeting Process Check

The Meeting Process Check focuses on what is happening in a meeting other than the content or specific agenda. The process scales reveal what areas are working well and what areas need the members' attention. After completing the Process Check scales, the team should discuss what process areas need to be improved.

On each of the following scales, place an "x" at the point that you believe best describes this session.

1. The general group atmosphere was:

    Relaxed ⬚⬚⬚⬚ Tense

2. Our objectives in this meeting were:

    Clearly stated ⬚⬚⬚⬚ Inadequately defined

3. The problem was:

    Easy to change, flexible ⬚⬚⬚⬚ Rigid, Inflexible

4.  Our methods in meeting our objectives were:

Helpful ☐☐☐☐ Dominating

5.  The leader appeared:

Involved ☐☐☐☐ Uninvolved, detached

Calm ☐☐☐☐ Agitated

Secure ☐☐☐☐ Insecure

6.  Most members of the team were:

Interested ☐☐☐☐ Bored

Participating ☐☐☐☐ Silent

7.  Participation in conversation was:

Evenly distributed ☐☐☐☐ Monopolized by a minority

8.  The quality of work accomplished was:

High ☐☐☐☐ Low

9.  Compared to other meetings of this team, this meeting was:

More effective ☐☐☐☐ Less effective

## Feedback: Giving and Receiving

| **Purpose** | Feedback helps others understand the impact of their behavior and ensures that learning takes place. It helps create positive experi- |

ences, focuses people's energies, and encourages people on their learning journey.

| **How to Use This Tool** | Use of this tool is straightforward, as de- scribed on the following pages. Remember that the feedback giver is speaking her or his |

truth about the *behavior* of the feedback receiver. Feedback does not infer intent. It should be given as soon as possible after the referenced behavior occurs. If it concerns a sensitive issue, feedback may be best delivered in private. However, the building of trust required for team development is enhanced when team members feel free to give open, honest feedback before the entire team.

| **Benefits** | Feedback is powerful and can increase productivity and morale. It allows for learning and behavior change. |

| **Pitfalls** | The recipient may become defensive. One avoids this pitfall by taking great care to be perceived as being helpful and by telling the truth without |

blame or judgment.

| **Story Application** | The story has numerous examples of both positive and negative feedback being given and received. George provides one outstanding example (page 46). |

> "He's not going anywhere. Besides, pay attention, please. The downer wasn't the fact that you did it. The downer was the sad look on your face when you had to. As a matter of fact, his comment was about how much he learns from a good fight like that. It's probably part of his personality. I'd say, going back to this list, that you encouraged an appropriate level of participation by being open and inclusive. You certainly didn't need to run the show. Furthermore, I've always been uncomfortable with the idea of shared or distributed or rotating leadership until I saw you in action this morning. Several of the folks were doing the influencing at different times this morning. When you did the slam to Henry, that's probably an example of focusing the process and bringing closure when necessary. You had already allowed reasonable digressions. Your action brought us all back to the task at hand."

George adhered to the feedback model of situation, behavior, and impact.

*Feedback for Individuals*

When offering feedback, it must be perceived as helpful. Feedback allows a person to:

- Understand the information.
- Accept the information.
- Do something about the information.

When *giving* feedback, follow the Situation, Behavior, Impact (SBI) Model.

1. Situation: Identify when and where the behavior occurred.
2. Behavior: Cite specific behavior that was observable to you.
3. Impact: Describe the impact the behavior had on you.

Giving feedback in this model is:

- Behavioral, not evaluative.
- Specific, not general.
- Focused on something the person can change.

When *receiving* feedback, consider these suggestions:

1. Listen carefully.
2. Try not to become defensive; rather, mentally note questions or disagreement.
3. Paraphrase what you think you hear, to check your perception.
4. Ask questions to clarify your understanding when you are unclear or in disagreement. Paraphrase answers again.
5. Carefully evaluate the accuracy and potential value of what you have heard.
6. Ask others whom you trust for more information.
7. Try observing your own behavior and the reactions of others to it.
8. Do not overreact to feedback. Modify your behavior in suggested directions, then check the outcomes.

Three important questions concerning feedback you have received are:

1. Is it accurate?
2. Is it important?
3. Do I want to change?

### Feedback for Team Members

When *giving* feedback to team members:

- Identify the behavior you value in the working relationship.
- State what you would like to have changed.

Follow the SBI Model:

1. Situation: When the team met to discuss our research findings . . .
2. Behavior: . . . and you arrived an hour late,
3. Impact: I felt our effort had suffered by your lack of input.

Writing down your specific feedback for each team member, using the following format, may help you to be clear and succinct. Telling teammates what you value helps them to replicate beneficial behavior. Telling them what you would like them to improve allows them to choose what behavioral changes are in consonance with their intent.

NAME _____

"WHAT I VALUE ABOUT OUR WORKING RELATIONSHIP . . ."

Situation _____

_____

Behavior _____

_____

Impact _____

_____

"OUR WORKING RELATIONSHIP WOULD IMPROVE IF YOU WOULD . . ."

Situation _____

Behavior _____

Impact _____

_____

_____

# PRINCIPLE FOUR: BE OPEN TO OUTCOMES

When I let go of what I am, I become what I might be. When I let go of what I have, I receive what I need.

—John Heider

THE FINAL PRINCIPLE in influencing others is to *be open* to outcomes, not *attached* to outcomes. One's natural tendency is to push hard for one's own position. Success often comes from winning a point or guiding the team to a predetermined position. However, teams reach synergistic results only when the outcome is a blending of the whole rather than a stamp of approval on one particular position. Even when an individual's stated proposal is the ultimate solution, the team must own it as their unique and combined product in order to fully implement the actions called for by their decision.

At first, the Fulcrum team stumbles onto the results of openness (page 18).

Sometime later, Lois said, "It's amazing what a change in atmosphere can do. I never thought we'd get to so much agreement. The funny thing is, while what we've decided is quite different from what I had in mind, I like it much better. . . ."

Later, as Janice and Pat try to implement their learnings, they are more intentional about openness. By now they have discovered the principles, thanks to Andy's persistence, and can more clearly categorize what they are doing (page 54).

> "On a scale of 1 to 10, what's your estimate of success now?" Janice asked Pat as they met on the phone in their respective offices.
>
> "Well, after such a rocky start, I would have said 2 at best. You brilliantly modeled openness in the midst of the fray. Our conversation may have convinced them of what we really wanted. So, right now, I could be as optimistic as 6 or 7," replied Pat.
>
> "I think you're right. I want to call Andy and thank him for his additions to the list, and get this new information to the rest of our team of directors. I still don't think it's complete, though."
>
> "It's too long already. What do we need to add?" Pat asked somewhat wearily.
>
> "Leadership can be learned. However, it's hard to do because you can't practice in the basement. You have to do it right in front of the people you want to lead," Janice observed. "You and I are demonstrating that now, at least to ourselves."
>
> "I guess that means we'll have to put up with a little embarrassment as we learn," returned Pat.

Pat is exactly right. Fear of being embarrassed because of not knowing all the answers or the specific outcomes creates the desire to be closed rather than open. The three tools in this section are designed to assist in being open to outcomes.

## Stop/Start/Continue

| Purpose |

This three-step model generates data by concentrating on what works well, what doesn't work well, and what needs to be done differently. This focus clarifies what tasks need to be accomplished and enables team members to remain open to outcomes. It creates a benchmark by showing the starting point for change efforts and for improvement of the organizational climate.

**How to Use
This Tool**

 There are a number of ways to implement this tool. The simplest is for team members to individually list specific actions they would like the team to stop, start, and continue. The respective lists are then combined. Prior to the development of trust within the team, one may choose to have a neutral person combine the lists anonymously. As the team builds trust, the input can be combined by verbal discussion. Once all input is received and items are clarified, action planning on what to do with the data is begun.

**Benefits**

 This simple approach to data generation, with appropriate follow-through, leads naturally to commitment to the resulting action plans. Such use helps create a learning team.

**Pitfalls**

 This exercise may feel contrived when it is initiated. It requires time and analysis. This pitfall can be avoided through visible and open implementation of the results. The stop/start/continue method is not a one-time effort, but is used continually for improved performance and learning.

**Story
Application**

 Although the Fulcrum team did not actually use this tool, there are several potentially applicable places in the story. The team of directors might have chosen to use it as a way to frame their task when they first met. This would have resulted in a more efficient understanding of how each member saw the problem. The tool may also have been useful to put anxiety or animosity to rest at the conclusions of activities. For example, when Henry responds (page 40):

> "... I have to be part of this task force because I have twice as much experience with having cooperation stuffed in my ear by the folks in that directorate. I wouldn't trust them with my worst enemy, let alone the data we're developing out of our latest research effort. This is the craziest idea I've heard in a decade. Don't you directors remember anything about organizational history?"

Henry is clearly telling the truth, but he is hardly "without blame or judgment" and is not very open to outcomes. If the conclusion of the "cooperative" ventures he mentions had been punctuated by a stop/start/continue exercise, he may have been more willing to work with these individuals in the future, knowing that both functional and dysfunctional behaviors (see Assessing Team Behavior, page 111) had been identified.

## The Process

The following questions can be asked of individuals and the answers anonymously compiled, or they can be asked within the team as a whole to allow open discussion of the responses. The specific wording can be changed in any way that makes sense to the team and taps specific areas of interest. Additional questions may help to develop each topic and assist in planning action based on the results of the exercise.

1. What are we doing that we should *stop?*
   - What actions are impeding individual, team, or organizational success in achieving the organizational mission?
   - Is there a compelling individual, team, or organizational reason for these actions?
   - Is the reason compelling enough to compensate for the negative effects of the action?
   - If the action is stopped, will the individual, team, or organization suffer?
2. What are we not doing that we should *start?*
   - What behaviors should be initiated to facilitate individual, team, or organizational learning?
   - What would create more successes, more productivity, more quality, and more enjoyment in the work of the individual, team, or organization?
   - Is there a compelling individual, team, or organizational reason for not taking this action?

- Is the reason compelling enough to compensate for the negative effects of not taking the action?
- If the action is started, will the individual, team, or organization suffer?

3. What are we doing that we should *continue?*
   - What actions have been accomplished that can be celebrated?
   - What actions are contributing to the success of the individual, the team, and the organization that should be continued?
   - How do these actions help achieve individual, team, and organizational success?

The answers to these questions provide the outline for an action plan. The team should discuss the answers and chart those responses that have a consensus. Under each category of stop, start, and continue, the actions are prioritized, beginning with the first issue to be addressed. One criterion for prioritizing is to select those actions that provide observable results in a short time frame. This method helps to reinforce the success of the process.

To ensure success, each action should be assigned to an individual who will coordinate completion of the issue, perhaps with a team of interested others. A time line for action and a procedure for reporting results will assist the team members in holding each other accountable.

Issues can be worked sequentially or simultaneously, depending on the size of the team, the magnitude of the issues, and the interest of the members.

## Asking Open Questions

| Purpose |

To be an effective communicator, the speaker needs to develop the ability to see how things look to the other person. This facilitates understanding. Open questions help to enhance communication and avoid incorrect assumptions, leading to the search for common ground among team members.

| **How to Use This Tool** | Any team member can ask open questions when conversation is at an impasse or positions are unclear. The questioner should take a |

moment to ask the question silently, being sure that the respondent cannot answer the question in one word. The question should honestly seek information without putting the respondent on the defensive about her or his position.

| **Benefits** | Open questions help create clarity and mutual understanding. They also help team members overcome unspoken barriers. |

| **Pitfalls** | The questioner may be perceived as too open and indecisive. To overcome this barrier, it is helpful to state explicitly that one is interested in the |

other person's point of view, and that the questioner is willing to express her or his position when appropriate.

| **Story Application** | An example of avoiding the pitfall is provided in the story (page 30). |

"OK, I guess a little humor is acceptable," Janice chimed into the conversation. "What do you mean by the next bullet? 'Mutual respect, willingness to listen, and trust come only after much work together.' I respected everyone here before we started. That's one reason I felt optimistic about the team from the beginning."

Here, Janice asks an open question, and before Andy has a chance to answer, she states her own position. One must assume that the tone of the conversation is not threatening. Given the context, it is clear that Janice is truly interested in Andy's response.

## Asking the Questions

The questions and the way they are asked determine whether the questioner will:

- Create or avoid potential conflict.
- Get all possible facts or just sketchy information.
- Turn off the person being questioned or establish mutual trust.

Open questions cannot be answered yes or no. Open questions invite an expression of opinion and feelings. For example:

How do you feel about . . . ?
What does . . . mean to you?
What do you think of . . . ?
What's your view of . . . ?
Can you give me an example of . . . ?

Open questions help achieve clarity and mutual understanding by:

- Creating interest in the other person; often, people are flattered when others are interested in them and in what they think.
- Making the other person more comfortable and secure because that person is placed "in the driver's seat."
- Asking for opinions and explanations in a nonthreatening way.
- Allowing more learning about the other person and what is on that person's mind; the answers often expose the real blocks to understanding.

Open questions are appropriate whenever one is interested in another person's opinion, or a discussion seems to have reached a roadblock. If a conflict appears imminent and the speakers have no apparent common ground, open questions may reveal commonalities on which the speakers can build consensus. Obtaining information from others is a key way of learning, and more information creates better decision making.

## Learning through Dialogue

| Purpose |
|---|

Complex environments require teams to explore issues from many points of view, going beyond individual and status quo thinking. Dialogue helps team members learn faster and smarter and enables teams to think *together*, both generatively and creatively.

| How to Use This Tool |
|---|

Use of this tool requires thinking "outside the box." Asking Open Questions (page 131) that are directly counter to one's own opinion is a helpful way to consider other points of view and creative options. The use of a facilitator may increase dialogue when team members are entrenched in individual points of view. Facilitators need not be content experts but should be skilled in process facilitation.

| Benefits |
|---|

Dialogue sensitizes team members to their own and the team's mental assumptions that form patterns of thinking. This breakthrough process allows consideration of options that might otherwise be dismissed. Learning through dialogue allows a team to go beyond its own limited perspective.

| Pitfalls |
|---|

By consciously engaging in dialogue, teams may slow down the problem-solving process by staying open for too long. To avoid this pitfall, team members must be conscious of realistic deadlines for moving ahead with their work, perhaps even without complete information.

| Story Application |
|---|

Janice and George engage in dialogue as they process the just-ended meeting (page 47):

"... but I still don't understand why everyone was so negative at first. How could that have been prevented? The atmosphere felt threatening to me. What is so threatening about excellence?"

"Nothing's threatening about excellence to these folks. What's threatening is elimination of redundancy. How would you feel if Gary said to you that he wanted redundancy eliminated, and you felt like the redundant one?"

"I never thought about it like that," admitted Janice. "We'd better call them back and tell them their jobs aren't in jeopardy."

The purpose of dialogue is to go beyond an individual's thinking and to gain and build insight from the team as a whole. Dialogue comes from the Greek *dialogos*, suggesting "meaning flowing through," as a stream flows—rushing and meandering on its course between two banks. Dialogue invites not a singular view but the views of all those present. It considers the whole stream— the banks, the source, and the destination. It acknowledges the whole system in addition to examining the separate elements that make the whole.

As dialogue develops, perhaps beginning as a conversation, it demands that participants pay attention to what is being expressed. Polarized opinions or assumptions may easily be taken for granted. Dialogue requires that people suspend judgment, let go of hard, foregone conclusions, and be open to explore others' views, as well as their own, in a spirit of inquiry.

It is useful to distinguish between dialogue and discussion. In *discussion* (which has the same root as percussion or concussion), teams look for alternate solutions. Through *dialogue* ("meaning flowing through"), teams acknowledge alternate views but go on to explore completely new perspectives.

### Steps to Starting a Dialogue

### 1. Suspend Assumptions and Certainties

Team members need to question and observe underlying assumptions for the purpose of awareness, not defensiveness. The discipline of suspending assumptions must be practiced by the whole team, allowing the members to see their own assumptions more clearly as they are held up for the scrutiny of others as well. All must try to avoid the delusion that "this is the way it is."

The natural tendency is to try to find the right solution, to fix the problem, or perhaps even to withdraw from the conversation. To practice dialogue is to continue to listen and inquire. Asking the following questions facilitates dialogue:

- How should I interpret what I'm hearing?
- What greater insight might come if I suspend judgment, if I don't attack?
- How am I listening?
- How might a different pace (perhaps slower) affect my listening and that of the team?
- What am I feeling? What might others be feeling?

## 2. Consider Each Other as Colleagues

Team members must see each other as colleagues if dialogue is to occur. Seeing another as a colleague requires a level of mutual respect and trust that often is found at later stages of the team development process. Learning through dialogue requires some self-disclosure and risk-taking, which is more comfortable in the presence of colleagues. Spending time getting to know one another and finding common assumptions, values, and goals is a valuable first step in initiating the behavioral tool of learning through dialogue.

## 3. Use a Skilled Facilitator

Because reliance on rank, the safety of nondisclosure, and unbalanced power relationships can inhibit dialogue, a skilled facilitator may be necessary. A skilled facilitator can promote an atmosphere of open inquiry and suspended judgment. The facilitator is not an expert, but a model who influences the flow of dialogue and encourages full participation. As a team becomes skilled in the art of dialogue, the facilitator is no longer needed. Skilled facilitators may be available within organizations or as consultants. Facilitation requires that the person remain neutral as to the content or outcome of the discussion at hand, in order to invite maximum participation and points of view.

# POSTSCRIPT

Team learning is a never-ending process of give-and-take. In a task-oriented organization, one strives to complete the project, accomplish results, and check off the completion. For teams, one is never able to check off the completion of learning. The human dynamics of team membership demand continuous attention to the processes of team development, trust, empowerment, and high performance.

Teams may use the tools in this book to aid their continuous learning through their own team development process. The tools are available for any team member to use and for all team members to discuss. They lead to self-improvement and progress toward high performance.

The tools apply to teams that meet only occasionally or those that work together daily. Conscious application of them may feel awkward initially. However, the more often one practices the use of these behaviors, the more comfortable one will become with their benefits, their pitfalls, and the appropriate times to use them to improve learning.

Learning teams are exciting, changing, high-performing teams that practice the honest and open dialogue of growth. The results of their work together are proof enough of the value of continuous learning for teams.

# $\mathscr{A}$BOUT VIMA INTERNATIONAL

VIMA International, The Leadership Group, is a firm of senior consultants who specialize in organizational, team, and individual leadership consulting. Event-based consulting includes large scale behavioral business simulations which assess individual leader behaviors, team learning activities, as well as organizational culture. VIMA International conducts organizational strategic planning and search conferences and works with partners within an organization to implement the vision and plan. Strategies and programs focus on performance, learning, and productivity to assist organizations undergoing technological, cultural, and structural change. The result is improved quality and profitability.

With offices in Virginia, Europe, and South Africa, VIMA International is an interdisciplinary team of consultants with line management experience and recognized academic credentials. Consultants have expertise in public and business administration, organizational behavior, industrial and clinical psychology, and human resource development. Clients include Atlantic Richfield Company (ARCO), HFSI, Life Technologies, Lockheed Martin Corporation, MCI Communications, The MITRE Corporation, NASA, PRC, Prudential, Scudder Stevens & Clark, Transnet, and The Vanguard Group.

# The Light Bulbs for Leaders Workshop

Based on the tenets of the light bulbs in *Light Bulbs for Leaders,* this workshop is an experiential approach to the development of learning teams. Participants will experience themselves as a learning team through an interactive process. The workshop allows discovery of both task and relationship behaviors necessary for learning team development. The workshop then involves participants in practicing the specific task and relationship skills that produce successful learning teams.

The workshop covers the five stages of team development, the four principles of leadership and learning, and the thirteen tools covered in the learning team problem matrix.

Participants will learn to understand team development and productivity. They will utilize the matrix of team problems and practice the particular skills to remove roadblocks of team development. They will leave with personal action plans to implement learning teams in their own work situations.

VIMA International, Inc.
5290 Lyngate Court
Burke, Virginia 22015
(703) 764-0780
Email: vimaint@aol.com

# $\mathcal{A}$BOUT THE VIMA LOGO

The graceful VIMA symbol is in the shape of an open circle. The arrow springs forth from the circle, in the direction of the mission of VIMA. It represents the strong nature of this organization, devoted to discovering a harmony, a set of goals, a philosophy, and a congruent business strategy as the solutions to clients' problems.

The heavy line on the left represents the needs of the client. The shape and arrow in the VIMA circle join with the clients' needs to form a new and successful direction. The open arrow at the bottom of the circle reflects the heavy arrow above, recognizing the lessons of the past which form the basis for an organization's values, culture, and essence. The openness of the circle allows input from the world so the organization functions as an open, changing, and learning system.

The word "Vima" is the Greek word for "pace," signifying the motto of VIMA International: *"Setting the pace for high performance."*

# INDEX